Spiritual Breath
The Practice of Kriya Yoga

Konstantin Serebrov
Gouri Gozalov

Serebrov Boeken Publishing
The Hague

© Publishing House Serebrov Boeken, The Hague, 2007
Telephone/Fax: +31- 70-352 15 65
E-mail: serebrovboeken@planet.nl
Website: www.serebrovboeken.nl

The English translation of a Russian book 'Практика Крийя-йоги' by Konstantin Serebrov, Moscow, 2006

Second edition

ISBN: 9789083267630; 978-90-832676-3-0

Editor:	Robin Winckel-Mellish, 'English Writers', Wassenaaar
Translators:	Gouri Gozalov and Maria Toonen
Illustraties:	Elena Obodova
Cover:	Gouri Gozalov

All rights reserved. No part of this publication may be reproduced or transmitted in any form or by any means, electronic or mechanical, including photocopy and recording, or stored in a retrieval system, without the written permission of the publisher.

Inhoudsopgave

Chapter 1. Meeting the first Mentor on the Path 6
Chapter 2. Getting out of the Body 13
Chapter 3. Meditation on the Mantra:
'I am the Radiance of the Absolute' 14
Chapter 4. A Place of Meditation in the Mountains 16
Chapter 5. Concentrating on the Mantra:
'I am an eternal Spirit' 18
Chapter 6. Concentrating on the Mantra:
'I am a spiritual Sun' 19
Chapter 7. The Necessity of Kriya Yoga
on the spiritual Path 20
Chapter 8. The spiritual Masters of Kriya 22
Chapter 9. Opening of the Chakras 25
Chapter 10. Five preparatory Meditations 31
Chapter 11. The Absolute, Creator of all Worlds 34
Chapter 12. The Meaning of Suffering 35
Chapter 13. Meeting with a Confederate Seeker
on the Path to the Absolute 37
Chapter 14. Slowing down the Breath
with the help of Prayer 39
Chapter 15. The Meaning of the sacred Sound 'Aum' 42
Chapter 16. Meditation on the sacred Sound 'Aum' 43
Chapter 17. The Kriya Technique 45
Chapter 18. Auxiliary Exercises 49
Chapter 19. Achievements on the Path of Kriya 54
Chapter 20. Waking of the Kundalini, or Snake Power .. 59
Chapter 21. The Technique of waking up Kundalini 62
Chapter 22. Samadhi 63
Chapter 23. The State of Super-consciousness 65
Chapter 24. A Gift from the Goddess Sarasvati 66
Chapter 25. A Message from the higher Worlds 69
Chapter 26. The Suggestions of Sri Yukteswar 75
Chapter 27. Praying to the Holy Trinity 84
Chapter 28. Practice in the Woods 86
Chapter 29. A Prayer to Lord Jesus Christ 88
Chapter 30. A Prayer to Mahavatara Babaji 89

Chapter 31. God's Voice 90
Chapter 32. Babaji Mahavatara and Babaji from Handakar 92
Chapter 33. Kasyan's Experiments
with the Kriya Technique.. 93
Chapter 34. Prayer to our Heavenly Father 97
Chapter 35. Contact with the Absolute
through the Third Eye... 99
Chapter 36. Meditations on the Images
of Mahavatara Babaji and Sri Yukteswar 102
Concluding Remarks from the Author 105
Endnotes.. 107

Chapter 1. Meeting the first Mentor on the Path

A boy called Kasyan was born in a small town in the Caucusus region of Russia, called Teberda, situated in a beautiful mountainous valley divided by a river with sparkling blue water, the source of which can be found high up in the mountains.

Even as a baby Kasyan had an irresistible desire to climb, and his parents often found the one year old sleeping quietly on the top of a high wardrobe.

The large windows of his room looked out in a southerly direction, and the sky above seemed to be calling him, and on clear nights he would gaze up at the shining stars above the mountain ridges for hours, as if he felt their magical attraction.

When Kasyan was three years old, his parents sometimes left him in the evenings in the care of an eighty year old woman who lived next door. They were young and liked to go to the cinema. 'If something scares you,' instructed his mother when leaving, 'just knock on the wall and granny will come.' One evening when Kasyan's parents were out and he was alone and still awake at midnight, he lay in his bed staring at the white wall opposite him and noticed to his amazement shining concentric circles on the wall. The circles resembled waves on the surface of a pond when a stone is thrown into the water. Gradually the circles became a maelstrom, and the space around started to vibrate, while in the centre of the maelstrom a passage appeared. Kasyan watched, as if enchanted, until he felt that he was being dragged into the maelstrom. 'A few seconds more," thought Kasyan, 'and this stream will drag me into some other unknown world, and I will never be able to find my way back home!' The thought terrified Kasyan and he started to bang on the wall with his small feet, calling for the old woman, realizing that by the time the old woman, who walked very slowly, reached his room, he could have already disappeared! With this thought in mind, Kasyan, dressed only in his underpants and vest, quickly climbed up to the small window above, which was partly open, and fell into a deep snow-drift under the window. Floundering desperately in the snow, he climbed out of the snow-drift and onto the small path near the house and, shivering from the cold, ran to the porch where he saw the old woman trying to open the door of his flat.

'For heavens' sake, what are you doing here?' she exclaimed when she saw a half-naked Kasyan covered in snow. 'I don't want to go back home,' said Kasyan in a trembling voice. The old woman took him into her flat, wiped off the snow, wrapped a warm blanket around him and put him in the chair beside the burning stove. She gave Kasyan a Bible to keep him quiet and he thumbed through the book with worn pages with great interest. It seemed to him that he was on the point of understanding the meaning of the words, printed in beautiful decorative letters. He felt attracted to the atmosphere of the Bible and it quietened him.

When Kasyan was eleven he stared at a twinkling star in the Orion constellation so intently as he lay in his bed one night, that its powerful energy dragged him out of his body. Kasyan sped into the starry space towards the unknown, like a comet, and enjoyed the flight, but when he looked back he saw to his horror that the earth was a shining hazy blue ball far away below him. The thought that he could be dragged into another constellation was very frightening, and he tried with all his power to slow down the speed of his flight. His new body looked exactly the same as his old body, which lay on a bed in one of the houses in a town in the mountains. Even though he had very little control, he managed to slow down his speed and felt that the thin shining thread between his new and his old body was strained to the limit. He realized that if he flew further the thread would break and he would be lost forever in the cold cosmos, between unknown planets. He would not be able to return to his home, which was fading into the distance. Fear made him focus fully on his will power, and suddenly he stopped. The thin shining thread, drew him like a stretched spring, back into his physical body which jerked a little from fear and tension.

Soon after Kasyan found a new friend, his classmate Youri, and they enjoyed strolling together in the mountains around the city, swimming in the river and fishing for trout. Sometimes when Kasyan came to visit Youri, he would warn Kasyan that they had to play very quietly, as his father was busy, and even the slightest noise would irritate him. Kasyan once, out of curiosity, glanced through a chink in the doorway, and he could see Youri's father, a grey-haired man, sitting with his legs crossed in the corner of his room. His eyes were fastened on a point between his eyebrows and he gave the feeling of complete serenity. This caught Kasyan's imagination and he was spirited away to the top of a crag where he saw himself sitting in the same strange posture, looking at the rising sun while an invisible sun flared up inside his chest. Even his heart stopped beating from an unknown joy.

'Do not disturb my father during his meditation,' Youri whispered in an irritated voice, dragging Kasyan away from the door. 'It is because of these meditations that he had to move to the Caucusus, in order to hide from the authorities.'

Kasyan really wanted to learn the art of meditation from Youri's father, and when he heard that Alexei was his name, he ran up to him and said timidly: 'I saw you sitting in an unusual posture. I would like to learn to sit like you and gaze at the point between the eyebrows.'

'You had better be careful,' said Alexei sternly. 'Otherwise they might expel you from school and send you to a reformatory. You don't need to learn this, its for adults, so that they can be relieved from the stress of work.'

'He probably thinks I'm an imbecile!' thought Kasyan, but he did not object and just nodded approvingly. 'I will have to nag him,' he concluded.

Kasyan began to follow Alexey during his evening walks, and pleaded with him to accept him as his disciple. Alexey always changed his route, but each time Kasyan managed to track him down and followed him, though keeping a distance.

After a year, Aleksey stopped, called Kasyan and told him: 'I'm tired of you following me. It would be easier , to teach you yoga rather than trying unsuccessfully to hide from you. Remember however, a yoga teacher is different from the usual kind of teacher. A yoga teacher acts as a mediator between the person and the higher worlds. I am not your teacher in this sense, but I will try to teach you at least a little. You can come to me tomorrow.'

Kasyan was very happy to become a disciple, even though not a real one, and every day he tried to learn from Alexey: he studied the yoga postures, crossed his legs in the lotus posture, and concentrated on the point between his eyebrows for an hour every day.

Kasyan's mentor taught him much, and he lent Kasyan a book by Edward Shure, called: 'The Great Initiates'. Kasyan tried to grasp the meaning of each word in this wondrous book, and absorbed the information in his soul. After he had read the chapter about Jesus Christ, he was very impressed and lay on his bed, thinking about the Lord Jesus Christ. Then he felt a wave of the highest love coming from Him, as though the heavens opened for an instant, and the unspeakable love of the Saviour, God's gift, touched him for a moment. From then on Kasyan was firmly convinced that everything that Shure had written about the coming of the Saviour was true, and Kasyan made even more of an effort to quickly ascend the ladder which leads to heaven.

Two years later when Kasyan turned fourteen, he earnestly questioned the meaning of his life, and the question he put to himself was: 'How can I make the most out of my incarnation?'

'What can I achieve if I became a scientist?' Kasyan thought. 'I will have a doctor's degree, and I will gain the respect of other people and earn good salary. I might even become an academic. However, I will have to study different sciences and will have to work at least twelve hours a day. When I am old my life will be joyless, and when my soul departs from my body, I will most probably sink into the lower worlds.

On the other hand I can follow the example of my uncle, who became a Communist Party functionary and is a close collaborator of Brezhnev. If I become like him I will gain honour and respect. But then again I will have to work at least ten hours a day, and, after my death, just as in the case of a scientist, I will fall into the lower astral worlds.

If I look at the examples of those who follow the Path in order to be able to communicate with God, I see that they spend about 10-12 hours a day on their practices. Contact with God gives them the highest love and also eternal bliss, and when their soul departs from the body, they go to the Heavenly Kingdom. Such an achievement is a thousand times more interesting than any achievement of an academic or a high-ranking communist.

When Yogis find contact with the Creator of the universe, they enter a state of super consciousness, or samadhi; as they discover the whole universe in their souls and they feel divine love and find eternal bliss.

So, the amount of time one needs for good results in these three directions is more or less the same. Only impractical people spend time during their incarnations doing things of minor importance. I will be practical and will spend my time in this incarnation by trying to enter a state of super consciousness. I don't think any of my relatives will support the idea; its more likely they will consider me a day-dreamer, or an idiot. My grandfather, however, was a rebel in the family as he followed his own conviction. Although he was a member of the gentry, he believed, for an unknown reason, in revolution. He sold his property and set up an underground printing-house, where he printed and distributed the works of Lenin in Moldavia. He could have certainly become prime minister if it were not for the chistka[1] in the Party in 1937 and the intrigues of his comrades-in-arms!

Children inherit a lot of their ability from their grandparents, and for this reason I do not lack persistency. It's clear to me that all people around me live according to the will of others, and not according to their own will. Parents instruct their children how to behave; school teachers teach us how we should live, office managers make their subordinates work. Only a small minority do what they really want, and the rest do what they are forced to do. For me, however, to live my incarnation according to the will of someone else, is just the same as living in vain. It would be better to die on the spot, because otherwise I will suffer by obeying the will of some strange unknown person, and what for? So I wish to live my incarnation according to my own will and do what I want to do, and not what others tell me to do! In addition, I have an average capacity as far as science and art is concerned, and it is unlikely that I would ever be successful in these areas. Also, I have no inclination to practise any kind of sport whatsoever! On the other hand my meditations and contact with the world behind the curtain are very successful. I meditate regularly two or three hours a day and meditation teaches me all that I need; and I have achieved the results promised in the books. Alexey and his friends, however, meditate for no longer than half an hour a day and then they spend hours discussing how splendid it would be if they met such a great teacher as Moria! Apparently the portrait of Moria is to them a representation which they honour, whereas when I look at it I see that his image radiates fire which affects my soul and burns there. I think I would rather develop and use this strange mystical talent of mine which nobody really understands, to obtain the best result possible: communication with God.'

After Kasyan took this decision, he started to meditate and to practise yoga even more. He stood on his head for an hour every day, in order to strengthen the blood vessels in his brain, so that when his kundaliny awoke and rushed upwards, the blood vessels would be able to stand the abrupt increase of blood pressure.

Soon after his parents divorced, Kasyan's father left for Kishinev, to live with his new wife and Kasyan remained with his mother until he finished his secondary school studies. He then joined the new family of his father in Kishinev, and prepared for the mathematical exam at the Kishinev University. His father lived with his second wife and her old mother in a one-room flat, as was customary in those times. Kasyan practiced his forty five minute-cycle of Yoga asana every morning on the only free spot in the flat, which happened to be right in front of the bathroom door in the corridor. After the asanas, he stood on his head for half an hour. From time to time he had to interrupt his postures in order to let the others into the bathroom. However, despite this inconvenience, Kasyan continued his practices.

Kasyan's father did not approve of his exercises. As the chief accountant of the National Theatre of Opera and Ballet, he did not approve of anything irrational, and gradually everyone in the flat had only one thing on their minds: how to get rid of Kasyan? The problem seemed to be solved when his father found a new one-room apartment, as he wanted to move there with his wife and leave Kasyan with the old woman. But the old lady flatly refused to live with Kasyan. 'I cant stand it anymore when this madman stands on his head everyday,' she said. Kasyan's father then took King Salomo's decision, and when he received the key of his new apartment he gave it to Kasyan.

After becoming the proud owner of the apartment, Kasyan immediately started to transform it into an ashram of a Yogi ascetic. He covered all the walls of the flat with the photos of the spiritual teachers, such as the Masters Moria, Kuthumi, Sivananda, Ramana Maharshi, Vivekananda, Ramakrishna and others, with pictures of the deities of the Hindu 'pantheon'. He pasted the portrait of the teacher Moria on the ceiling right above the head of his bed, and made a secret cell for meditation in the small pantry. He fastened sound insulating mats on the walls and on the door, and covered everything with blue silk. He also put a safe lock on the door.

'Now I can live exactly as I please,' reasoned Kasyan. 'The next thing to do is to collect as much information about the spiritual practices as possible,' he thought and phoned an old friend of Alexey, called Andrey, who was a mystic from Moscow. Andrey had been collecting esoteric books for more than forty years, and said that Alexey had told him about Kasyan, and he invited him to visit.

Kasyan stayed in his uncle's flat as the high ranking family were residing in their summer residence, and Andrey showed Kasyan around his library and told Kasyan to choose any title. Kasyan selected ten titles and Andrey gave him films that Kasyan had to process. 'The books about spirituality,' Andrey said smiling sadly, 'are available in our country only in the form of xerox- or photocopies. This take so much time and money, but certainly forms mystics with stable characters.'

Kasyan printed several thousand photos with a rather blurred text in the photo laboratory of his cousin, and returned home with the new books.

CHAPTER 2. GETTING OUT OF THE BODY

Kaysan read all the books including 'The Mystics and the Magicians of Tibet' by Alexandra David Neel, and decided to learn the practice of astral exteriorisation, which is a way of getting out of the physical body. He tried all the different ways of getting out of one's body that he could find in the esoteric methods. but none of them worked properly and Kasyan decided to repeat a kind of inward mantra: 'I have to get out of my body,' which he repeated during all his usual daily pursuits in his unconscious mind. By now he had passed the examinations and had become a student at the mathematics faculty of the university. He studied mathematics gladly, but did not lose the intention to get out of his physical body.

Kaysan woke up late one night and felt that he had sunk into the green sofa on which he slept. 'This cannot be true!' he thought, and the next moment he found himself moving upwards, soaring above the sofa, on which he saw his own body lying motionless under a blanket. Kasyan flew up to the ceiling, looked down at his room in amazement, and then some power drew him effortlessly back into his body. The next morning Kasyan doubted whether he had really got out of his body, and his sceptical mind kept repeating that it was only a hallucination. Nevertheless, the next night he escaped from his body again, circled for a while, and then returned to his body which lay on the sofa. His consciousness was as clear as when he was awake, and he could remember everything, but in the morning his mind would once more not totally accept the experience. Kasyan left his body regularly, several times a week, and then he gradually learned to leave his body deliberately, using will power.

'I certainly know from my experience that I am not really my physical body,' thought Kaysan. 'Why then do I need to care for it so much when it is so unreliable and might die at any moment? Why do I need to study, make a career, and take part in a 'social life' which is based on the needs of the physical body? On the other hand, I do not know who I am. The only thing I do know is that I am a being which is aware of itself and can live in the physical body as well as outside it.'

CHAPTER 3. MEDITATION ON THE MANTRA: 'I AM THE RADIANCE OF THE ABSOLUTE'

One of the books that Kasyan borrowed from Andrey, was a book by Paul Branton about Ramana Maharshi. When Ramana was young, the question arose in his mind during a service in a Hindu temple: 'Who am I?' and he went into a deep meditation, waiting for an answer from the depth of his soul.

He retired to a cave on the mountain Arunachala, where he meditated on this question. When he received the answer he was enlightened, and gradually became a celebrated spiritual teacher. He had many disciples who tried to follow his example and Kasyan decided to become a follower of Ramana Maharshi as well, and regularly meditate while repeating: 'Who am I?' He concentrated on these words for hours, but still the answer did not come. Months passed and the summer vacation arrived and Kasyan managed to squeeze himself out of the obligatory work in the Kolkhoz vineyards for second year students, and went to his native town to visit his mother and ask Alexey about the meditative question: Who am I?

'I think,' Alexey explained, when Kasyan told him about his unsuccessful attempts, 'that Maharshi's meditation was successful because he spontaneously felt a contact with a Hindu goddess in the temple, who revealed to him the innermost secret of this meditation. 'What should I do?' asked Kasyan despondently.

'While concentrating on your heart during meditation,' Alexey answered, 'repeat the words: I am the radiance of the Absolute. Find a suitable place in the mountains, with pure vibrations which will support you spiritually. Sit in the lotus posture, close your eyes and recite inwardly: I am the radiance of the Absolute. Then your meditation will be more successful. You could find a cave, or a rock near the lake, on the top of a mountain or on the steep bank of the river.'

The sun was shining brightly the next morning, and huge white clouds hung close to the mountain tops when Kasyan decided to walk to the river bank. The mountain river rushed through the valley, winding between huge boulders and small groves. Kasyan picked a rock which seemed to attract him, sat down on it with his legs crossed, and concentrated on the point between his eyebrows. When his breathing slowed down, he started to recite slowly in his mind: 'I am the radiance of the Absolute.' Suddenly a strange rustle came from beside the boulder. Kasyan looked up crossly and saw a passionate couple lying there. He went on reciting the mantra, keeping his concentration on the third eye. But the more he concentrated the louder the noise. Kasyan lost his patience, and after giving the indefatigable couple a disapproving glare, he left. 'I will have to look for a place of spiritual power somewhere in the mountains, far away from people,' he decided.

Chapter 4. A Place of Meditation in the Mountains

Kaysan woke up very early the next morning and started out for the marble cave, which was situated in a rather desolate and inaccessible place which nobody visited. The sun was barely visible behind the ridges by the time he had reached the blue marble cliffs and started to climb. Within a couple of hours he had reached a dangerous piece of rock which lay above the precipice, right in front of the cave. When he stepped onto it, a strong gust of wind nearly blew him off into the abyss. Kasyan had to lie on his belly and crawl towards the cave clutching at the roots of a juniper plant. The closer Kasyan got to the cave, the fiercer the gusts of wind became. It seemed as if the wind was alive and trying to drive him into the abyss. Fearing for his life he finally reached the cave, threw off his knapsack with the ropes and the food, and went to inspect the cave. The cave was no more than thirty meters deep and the entire floor was covered with the droppings of bats which hung threateningly from the ceiling. 'I am sure that nobody will disturb me in this cave,' said Kasyan rejoicing.

He could not find any rock snakes, or any other suspicious looking creatures, but a place with friendly vibrations, so he sat down with his legs crossed and immersed himself in meditation. The sharp smell of the bat's droppings at first did not allow him to concentrate on the mantra: 'I am the radiance of the Absolute', and when he finally managed to concentrate, he suddenly heard strange rumbling sounds coming from the dark end of the cave, resembling foot steps. No matter how hard Kasyan tried to convince himself that nobody could possibly be there, the more distinct the foot steps became, and he felt horror when he saw out of the corner of his eye a long shadow which was bowing over him threateningly. Without waiting, he stood up and ran to the entrance, but when he looked back, the space around looked quiet and peaceful again. 'I probably just imagined it,' Kasyan thought, and sat down by the entrance with a huge abyss before him. When he went into himself again, he suddenly felt as if somebody's invisible hands were trying to push him into the abyss. 'These are just hallucinations, caused by my fears,' he tried to explain to himself, but the atmosphere felt even more threatening. 'Obviously,' thought Kasyan, 'this is an invisible entity which occupies the cave and is hostile to my meditation. But I refuse to leave such a romantic place.' Kasyan left the cave, took a rope from his knapsack and tied one end around his waist, and the other to a lonely pine tree which grew on the edge of the abyss. 'Now nobody will be able to drive me away,' thought Kasyan, smiling to himself. He then sat down with his legs crossed on the hard roots protruding from the ground, and immersed himself in meditation, concentrating on the mantra: I am the radiance of the Absolute .When he heard angry and persistent foot steps on the rock above his head, Kasyan looked back cautiously but there was only a high cliff above him, without any living creature. He went into meditation again, repeating the mantra. The horrifying steps were approaching him, and again the invisible hands tried to push him into the abyss. Kaysan was panic stricken and with trembling fingers he untied himself from the tree and crawled back to the steep rock desperately clutching at the coarse juniper roots. The spirits of the air had angrily dishevelled his cloths, and had tried to push him into the abyss. He sat down and quietened himself, looked around and saw a suitable place for meditation up in the mountains. Within a couple of hours he arrived there and sat down on a flat stone to meditate. The worldly trivialities seemed insignificant on top of the mountain, and the presence of the Creator of all the worlds, the Absolute, was very real. Kasyan was pleased that after all his work he could experience such a detached, elevated state of mind. But after he had reached a complete silence of the heart, and was in meditation, a piercing, cold wind started to blow. 'How can the Tibetan ascetics meditate in mountain caves,' thought Kasyan. 'They must suffer terribly from the cold!' Soon his hand became blue and felt like ice. Kasyan confessed to being far weaker than the Tibetan monks and was not able to continue his meditation. He packed up his belongings and hastily descended the glacier. When he heard a strange rumble he looked back, and paralysed with fear saw a huge rock rolling down over the deep snow towards him. Kasyan threw himself to the right of it, but the stone hit something and also turned slightly inwards. Kasyan ran to the left, but the stone hit something again and veered off to the left. 'What the devil is going on!' Kasyan thought in panic, as he was less than ten metres from the stone. He pleaded to the Mother of God for help, and to his surprise the stone stopped at a distance of three metres from him. Kasyan quickly ran down to the lake and dived into the icy water. He came to his senses and returned home. He did not want to roam the mountains anymore in search of a solitary place to find spiritual power.

CHAPTER 5. CONCENTRATING ON THE MANTRA: 'I AM AN ETERNAL SPIRIT'

'I don't think,' Alexey said, when Kasyan told him about his adventures, 'that you are ready yet for the powerful mantra: I am the radiance of the Absolute. I suggest you try to concentrate on the words: I am an eternal spirit.'
Kasyan followed this advice and sat for hours in the lotus posture on the floor in his room concentrating on the mantra: I am an eternal spirit. After following this practice for a month, he felt a radiant, spiritual being during the meditation, who lived eternally in the cosmic space; a

bodiless being flying without any restriction into the cosmos. His consciousness still retained its clarity, and in addition, he was independent of his physical body and could soar like a bird, enjoying limitless freedom. Kaysan realized that he was immortal as the spirit is impervious to time. It was a gripping sensation and it aroused in him the wish to exercise the practises even more, and he told Alexey about his experience.

'I'm glad that you have become aware of your infinite nature,' his mentor commented.

'The question is, what are the possibilities for the free spirit? asked Kasyan a little anxiously. 'I now realize very clearly that worldly, earthly purposes do not make any sense.'

'You are perfectly right,' he answered, 'the only purpose of a spiritual being is to merge with the Absolute, the Creator of all the worlds. This is the most worthy purpose. And when this purpose is realized, when contact with the Absolute is found, the next task will arrive: to help the Absolute to realize the evolutionary process on the planet earth.'

'I can hardly believe that the Absolute would need anyone's help,' Kasyan remarked.

'These are the sleeping human souls, who need help,' said his mentor. 'They forget their spiritual nature and became identified so deeply with their physical body that they believe they will die together.'

CHAPTER 6. CONCENTRATING ON THE MANTRA: 'I AM A SPIRITUAL SUN'

'The next challenge to your growing consciousness would be to concentrate on the mantra: I am a spiritual sun,' said his mentor. 'Every human being has the radiant sparkle of the Absolute in his soul, which manifests itself as a transcendental, spiritual sun. Meditate on the sun, which is concealed in your spiritual heart, for two hours each day, and you will experience an elevated, mystical state that will rise up inside you,' concluded his mentor.

And so Kasyan sat in the lotus posture each morning, with his eyes closed, and concentrated on his spiritual heart, which lay in the middle of the chest and recited at the same time: 'I am a spiritual sun'. Kasyan concentrated on this mantra for many days without any result. But just when he had almost lost all hope, a vast golden sun flared up inside his chest. Its incredible radiance filled Kasyan's soul with unspeakable bliss. 'Now you know who you really are,' Alexey commented, when Kasyan told him about the meditation the next day. 'You are a small particle of the great Absolute, Whose image shines in your heart like the eternal spiritual sun. Again you have received proof that there is a spiritual Path which you should follow in order to realize your highest, spiritual nature.

These glimpses of super consciousness, however, are beautiful gifts from above. In order to become truly stabilised on such a level, you should first purify and transform your lesser polluted nature, in order to find God inside your heart. This is called the 'spiritual Path' and is a long and laborious period during which your soul and body is purified and prepared for communication with the great Absolute.'

'How can I learn about this?' asked Kasyan.

'I think the time has come to tell you about the practice of Kriya, which accelerates the spiritual growth of man,' answered Alexey.

Chapter 7. The Necessity of Kriya Yoga on the spiritual Path

Kriya Yoga is the quickest way of attaining spiritual freedom. What is appreciated is the fact that one does not need to renounce society or the family and go into seclusion, as was done in the past. You can carry out this practice and find God inside you, while still pursuing a normal family life and job. A spiritual seeker can lead a normal life, according to the generally accepted social codes, and still remain an investigator of the mysteries of his own inner depths. By using this technique, we can touch upon our highest Selves, which would be impossible in the usual state of consciousness.

Kriya was given re-birth by the great avatar Babaji, who lives for about a thousand years in the Himalayas, while preserving his physical body. It is said that when Babaji was a young boy of sixteen, he wanted to become a disciple of a great spiritual Master of Kriya, who lived for hundreds of years in the forests of the Himalayan mountains. He arrived in the area where, rumour has it, the dwelling place of the Master was located and he roamed the forest, calling loudly, but the Master did not respond. Babaji took an oath to God that he would sit in the forest without eating and drinking, until either the Master, or his death arrived. He sat in the lotus posture and beseeched the great Master to accept him as his disciple. Days passed and Babaji remained in complete solitude. After three weeks Babaji was completely exhausted from hunger and thirst, but still the Master did not respond. Nevertheless he did not give up and stayed there meditating and praying to God. On the twenty-eighth day he realized that he was about to die, but still he remained sitting, because he knew that without Kriya Yoga he could never find God, and without God his life had no meaning. So when death touched his shoulder, the great Master appeared before him and said: 'I watched you from the start, and now I am convinced that you are prepared to sacrifice your life in order to find God. You have proved to be worthy of studying with me.' For several decades the Master had been teaching Babaji the different methods of Kriya Yoga, and the secrets of the preservation of the physical body. The Master told Babaji that he had been given a special mission and that he would live on earth for many thousands of years. Babaji practised the Kriya techniques day and night, and after many years found God inside himself, and after merging with the Absolute, he became the great avatar of India. In the middle ages, during the civil wars in India, the secrets of this practice were lost. By the end of the 18th century

Babaji heard the call of many souls and decided to restore the practice of Kriya. For this purpose he chose a man called Lahiri Mahasaya and taught him the techniques of Kriya Yoga. Lahiri Mahasaya had many disciples, the best known being Sri Yukteswar Giri, who, in turn, transmitted the message of Kriya Yoga to the western world through his disciple, Yogananda.

CHAPTER 8. THE SPIRITUAL MASTERS OF KRIYA

'Please tell me more about the great teachers of Kriya,' Kasyan asked his mentor.
'Lahiri Mahasaya,' said Alexey, 'met his teacher, Babaji, when he was over thirty and already had a wife and children. Nevertheless, thirty years later he became the most well-known teacher of Kriya Yoga. He found contact with the great Creator of the universe and co-created with Him. He mastered the mystery of creation and of life and death. He found immortality, but he remained natural in his ways and he did not strive to become an object of worship or adoration. And who would have thought that he had started off as a clerk at a railway station burdened with a family!
Sri Yukteswar followed the example of his Master and reached spiritual perfection early. He also became a well-known spiritual teacher. This proves that the methods of the evolutionary practice of Kriya allows a simple man to reach spiritual perfection and find God within himself in one incarnation. Sri Yukteswar raised the snake power of kundalini, and having obtained full control over it, he reached the state of samadhi. However, as a young man he was just a simple and stubborn Hindu lad. Neither he nor Lahiri Mahasaya had any obvious talent in their youth; they were exactly the same as those around them - common Hindu men. They had just one, hidden talent: they firmly believed that the Kriya practice would elevate their consciousness. They were able, unlike others, to practise the spiritual breath regularly for many hours a

day. They took it as seriously as common people take the earning of money, and made the practising of Kriya their daily work. This practice changed them so deeply that they have become great spiritual teachers, known throughout the whole world.

Their families, their close relations and friends hardly noticed their transformation. Some of their friends had become successful businessmen, others were just employees who were forced to go to their jobs every day and support a family. But these two people were occupied with spiritual practice until they reached perfection and had become great teachers. What more proof do you need to realize that if you practise the Kriya techniques as passionately as they did, you will find God inside yourself? Like Lahiri Mahasaya, you will be able to vanish into thin air and reappear, experience the state of samadhi and the cosmic state of consciousness, communicate in the deepest silence with the divine Mother and find contact with the Creator of the universe. If you follow the example of these two, you will be also be able to reach spiritual perfection. Everything depends on how much effort you invest in the spiritual breath. There is nothing miraculous about these methods, just hard work on the transformation of one's consciousness.'

'What is the Kriya practice actually?' Kasyan asked.

The spiritual effect of the Kriya technique is based on a certain regularity, discovered by the ancient Hindu sages who were called rishi's. The total life energy of man makes a full circle during a year. Starting at the coccyx, it moves upwards along the spine to the third eye, at the point between the eyebrows. Then it turns around the third eye along the circular orbit, which lies approximately a centimetre outside the head, and returns into the head at the point approximately one centimetre above the third eye. Then it returns back into the coccyx along the rear side of the 'pipe' of the spine. While rotating around the third eye, which is connected to the divine worlds, the energy is purified and saturated with spiritual warmth.

In this way man grows spiritually and gradually comes closer to his Creator, the Absolute. Rishi calculated that when energy has made one million such rotations, that is after a million years, it would be fully spiritualised and man would naturally be able to merge with the Absolute. This was successfully proved through practice, that only one such rotation of energy, made deliberately with the help of a concentrated attention and special breathing, would spiritualise man's energy to the same extent as its natural rotation during an entire year! A simple reckoning shows that a year of daily practice would let his or her consciousness grow to an extent equal to 365,000 years of natural spiritual evolution. Such accelerated development is of course only possible for someone who is specially trained by his teacher. Such a person should train his body and mind for a long time, so as to be able to stand this practice. An ordinary person cannot endure the strong inner tension that the practice of Kriya causes. A Kriya practitioner who dies before he has reached complete inner liberation, preserves all his achievements in Kriya in the next life. In his new life he will obviously strive once more in his efforts to find God.

The practice of Kriya teaches one to slow down the breath, so that man needs less air. Gradually the heartbeat becomes slower and the life energy is pulled away from the muscles and inner organs and is concentrated in the chakras, causing them to open. Rishi used to say that the breath is like an invisible glue which keeps man's consciousness fixed on the matter. But if man makes breathing effortless, which happens naturally when we sleep, then man can be liberated from matter and enter into a state of super consciousness.

The practitioner of Kriya focuses his mind on his breathing and moves his energy up and down through his seven chakras, filling them with life power which is pulled from the body.

The chakras and their projections in the physical body are made up of:

1. Coccyx plexus – muladhara chakra
2. Sacrum plexus – swadhisthana chakra
3. Waist plexus – manipura chakra
4. Chest plexus – anahata chakra
5. Neck plexus – vissudha chakra
6. Medulla oblongata – adjna chakra
7. Brain – sahasrara chakra

The third eye, which is connected to the medulla oblongata, is to man the source of the living Spirit, just as the sun is the source of life for all living beings.

Chapter 9. Opening of the Chakras

Our soul is made up of several shells, all of which have different degree of coarseness. The roughest is our physical body; our astral body which consists of sheer energy and is the more subtle shell. The astral body looks like an exact copy of the physical body, and the astral brain, astral spine and the spinal cord are also to be found in the astral body. The astral spinal cord is the location of the seven mysterious chakras which feed our physical body with the energy that emerges from our heavenly Creator, and for this reason you cannot find chakras in the physical body.

The first chakra corresponds to the element of earth. Its physical projection is located in the coccyx and is thought to be a sacred chakra, as this is the dwelling place of the sleeping snake power called kundalini.

The second chakra has a physical projection and is located in the spine - four fingers above the muladhara chakra which corresponds to the element of water.

The third chakra is called manipura and is located in the spine in the area of the solar plexus. It corresponds to the element of fire.

The fourth chakra is called anahata. Its physical projection is located in the area of the spiritual heart on the spine, on the level of the physical heart. It corresponds to the element of air.

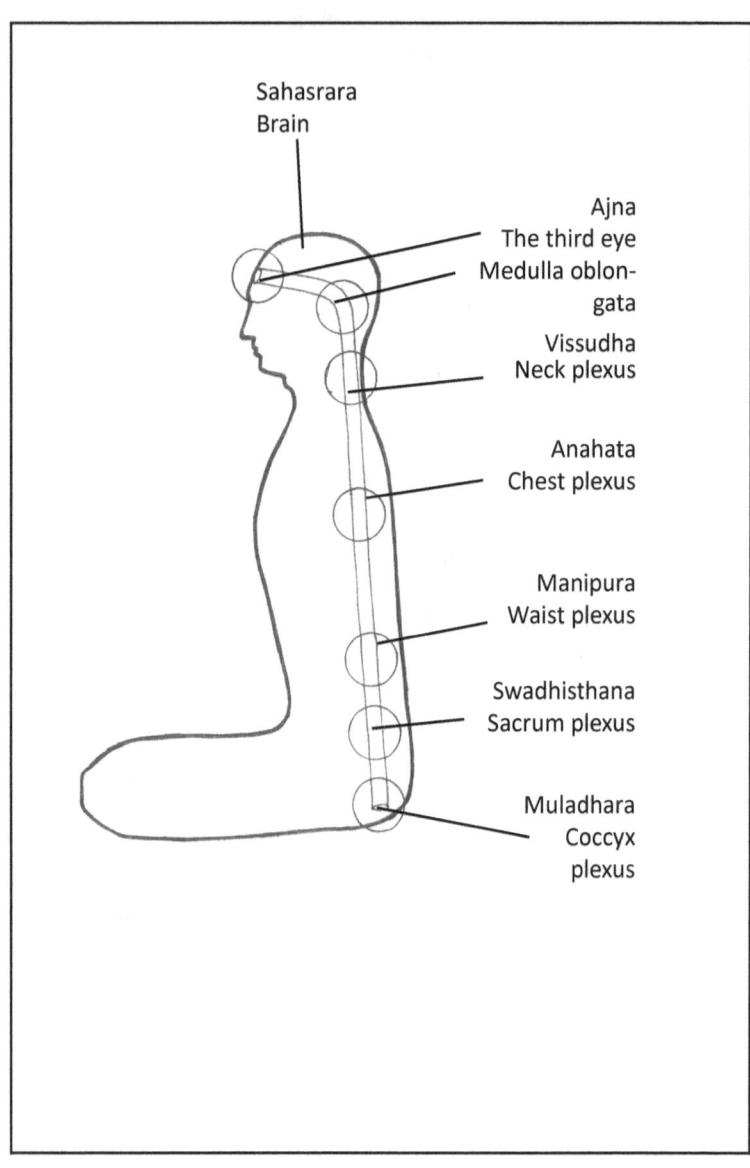

Illustration 2. The location of the plexuses in the body

The fifth chakra is called vissudha. Its physical projection is located in the vicinity of the neck of the spine, near the gullet plexus. It corresponds to the element of ether.

The sixth chakra is called adjna. Its physical projection is located in the medulla oblongata, at the part of the head above the top of the spine. This chakra accumulates our life power, or prana, in Sanscrit. It corresponds to the super ethereal element. The most subtle part of this chakra is the so-called third eye, which is located at the point between the eyebrows.

The seventh chakra is called sahasrara. Its physical projection is our brain, and when it opens it radiates a thousand white rays of prana, and man finds in his inner world the angels and God himself, the Creator of the universe. When all the seven chakras open, man hears the sacred sound Aum, which is produced by the energy which comes from the Absolute, and which supports the existence of the entire universe.

Cosmic energy first arrives in the medulla and is accumulated in the brain. Prana is then distributed by the six chakras in the spine and is consumed by the whole organism. The astral body is in fact a coagulation of the light energy which comes from the seven chakras.

Our entire body is constantly fed with astral energy which comes into the physical body through the medulla and is distributed there by the lower chakras. If we want to open our third eye, we must pull all the prana from our physical body back into the medulla. When this happens the body stiffens and becomes immobile, while the life energy in the medulla shines with a radiant light.

The seven chakras are very much like seven seals which seal the human soul in the physical body, and for man to escape his physical shell, he must open these seven seals.'

'How can I do this?' Kasyan asked.

'Exactly as I told you: you should pull the energy from your body into these chakras. They will open and you will leave your physical body and enter your subtle body.'

'But I have left my body so many times! Does this mean that I have at least opened a few of my chakras?' asked Kasyan.
'Yes, that is so, but you penetrate an astral plane, which is situated close to the earth. Such an exteriorisation does not contribute to your spiritual growth, on the contrary, it can become an obstacle to your spiritual growth and travelling into the lower astral worlds can be especially dangerous. Just like drugs they will burn all the reserves of the energy of your soul and then you won't be able to even to live normally, let alone experience spiritual growth!

Also, when your astral body leaves your physical body, it remains connected to the physical body by a thin cord which can stretch to a great extent. This cord is a kind of channel through which part of the divine energy still comes into the physical body. However, if this cord for some reason breaks, then the physical body will die. When an astral traveller arrives in the light astral worlds, he or she will not want to return to earth, but when they get into the dark worlds they will try with all their strength to get back into the physical body.'

'I always felt this cord when I left my body,' remarked Kasyan.

'When divine energy arrives in the manifested universe, that is our physical world,' Alexey went on, 'it reaches the astral medulla oblongata first, and then moves into the astral brain where it accumulates. The three astral channels which begin at the medulla are made up of the negative channel; the positive channel and the neutral, balancing channel. Passive, female energy flows along the first channel, while along the second channel flows male, active energy; while neutral androgynous energy flows along the third central channel. Passive female energy which comes from the cosmic moon feeds the human soul; active male energy which comes from the cosmic sun feeds human essence, and androgynous spiritual energy which flows along the central channel once more balances them. The central channel penetrates all the seven chakras into the astral spinal cord.

The human nervous system can stand only the impulses which come from the brain and the spinal cord, and would not be able to stand the 'voltage' of the spiritual current which comes from the Absolute, the Creator of all the worlds and would just burn through as domestic electric wiring when connected directly to a high-voltage line. The practice of Kriya, however, transforms and enforces the nerves and prepares them to conduct 'high-voltage', divine energy. It brings peace and regenerates the nerves of the spinal cord and gradually changes the structure of the astral body, so that when reaching the higher stages of this practice, you will be able to endure the cosmic energies which are involved in the process of the creation of the manifested worlds.

Most people live under the domination of the laws of maya, the great cosmic illusion. Their life energy is directed outwardly and is spent in living a common way of life and enjoying sensual pleasures. A Kriya practitioner offers his worldly aspirations to the altar of fire, and burns his karma in the inner fire of dedication to God. All his past and present wishes and desires become a fuel which is consumed by divine love. Its fire burns to ashes the negative karma which was caused by faults and wrong deeds, and the practitioner obtains divine wisdom. Babaji wanted all those who want to grow spiritually at a quicker rate, to use this practice to accelerate spiritual growth. Kriya practitioners can make contact with the Absolute in only one incarnation. They broaden their consciousness, open their higher centres and find their own Highest Self.

As Christians we aspire to our Lord Jesus Christ and the Kriya technique is another means of finding the Lord Jesus Christ in ourselves. Sri Yukteswar says that Babaji is deeply connected to Jesus Christ and helps Him in the process of divine creation.

The central, androgyne channel

The passive, female channel

The active, male channel

Illustration 2. The principal astral channels of man

By the end of the 19th century Babaji heard a call for help on the spiritual Path from many souls in the West, and for this reason he stimulated the spreading of the message of Kriya.

The more we open the higher inner centres of man, the more sensitive we are to the message of our Lord. A person whose higher centres are closed, will not hear God's answer when he prays.

When practising the Kriya technique, the energy will gradually flow away from the five senses and your heartbeat will slow down. The energy will be accumulated in your spine and the six chakras there will vibrate and will open. This is exactly the moment when your prayer to God will be very intense. The slowing down of your heartbeat and your breathing are the signs that you have obtained control over you life energy, or prana. Once this has been achieved you will be able to open a mysterious door inside your heart and communicate with God.

'On this note' the mentor concluded, 'I will end my story. Go home and try to write down all that I told you. Come tomorrow with a pen and a notebook, so that you can write down everything straight away.'

Kasyan thanked Alexey and went home. He felt as if he was soaring on invisible wings and he daydreamed about meeting with Babaji, Sri Yukteswar and the other Hindu teachers who would certainly become interested in him once he started practising Kriya.

CHAPTER 10. FIVE PREPARATORY MEDITATIONS

'Today we will go to an isolated lake,' said Alexey when Kasyan came to him the next morning. 'I will show you several meditations which will prepare your consciousness for the Kriya practice.'

When they reached the azure lake in a desolate valley, the mentor put his woollen blanket on the grass near the rock and sat down on it in the lotus posture. Kasyan put his blanket beside Alexey's, sat down on it and took out his pen and notebook.

'We think of ourselves as a bodily entity, almost from the moment of birth' Alexey said. 'We do not remember our spiritual nature, our soul. This is the hypnosis of maya, or illusion, which erases all the memories of our spiritual origin. The older we become the more difficult it is to get rid of this, and we become more and more convinced that we ourselves will die when our bodily shell dies. But this is not so, as we are created in the image of the heavenly Creator, and this means that we are all immortal, an eternally living, spiritual being. Our body perishes, but we live eternally.

A human being has a threefold nature which is made up of the body, the soul and the spirit. Our spirit is a heavenly fiery substance and manifests itself through the male origin. Our soul is a flowing female heavenly substance, and it envelops and softens our fiery spiritual origin. Our body is the container of our soul and spirit and gives us the opportunity to be active in the manifested universe. As our bodily sensations are not as subtle as our spiritual sensations, they stifle our soul and spiritual manifestations. So, in order to solve the riddle of the sphinx and become fully aware of ourselves, we should use special methods of concentration and meditation. These methods sedate our mind, emotions and bodily sensations, and we can perceive the subtle manifestations of our flowing soul and our fiery spirit. In order to prepare ourselves for these experiences, let us perform a simple exercise.

Sit with your legs crossed on a woollen blanket which isolates you from the negative energies of the environment. Straighten your spine so that the life energy can move freely up and down. Relax the muscles of your body, throw off all thoughts and emotions and immerse yourself in a state of inner peace. Begin to meditate on one of the themes which will help you to become aware of your higher nature.

Meditation 1.

'I am connected to God, who is the centre of the world; inside me there is a universe.' Sitting in the lotus posture, you should concentrate on your spiritual heart every day, which is located in the middle of the chest, while at the same time repeating this mantra. After several months of practice, an unbounded universe will eventually open inside you. You will be enraptured when you are able to see it outside as well as inside yourself. Thousands and thousands of suns, all the colours of the rainbow will shine inside you. You will realize that you are the centre of this universe.

Meditation 2.

'O Lord, your heart is one with the hearts of all human beings, and also mine. Lord, help me to become aware of this.'

We should love all people, because the Heavenly Creator is also the collective soul of the entire humanity. The closer we are to Him the deeper we merge with the entire manifested humanity. Meditate on the thought that your soul is one with all human souls, your mind and your heart are connected to the minds and the hearts of all the people on this planet.

Meditation 3. 'I am the spirit which radiates golden light.'

Imagine that, from the point between your eyebrows, which is the centre of the third eye, a gentle golden light emanates. This light fills your mind, penetrates your heart, and eventually fills your entire being until you are completely dissolved in the light. You will feel an unspeakable bliss as you feel as if you are golden light in a radiant infinity.

Meditation 4. Meeting with the Heavenly Father.

Imagine, at the point between your eyebrows, that a broad golden tunnel which leads to the higher worlds and to our Heavenly Father, appears. Fly, in your thoughts, through this tunnel at an enormous speed and reach the end, where you will find a huge, radiant golden sun. A penetrating voice from the centre of this sun will say: 'I have been waiting so long for your coming.'

This meditation will allow you to penetrate the supreme spiritual reality and meet our Heavenly Father.

Meditation 5. The two dwellings.

Try to feel the two dwellings. The first dwelling is the entire manifested cosmos in which we all dwell.

The second is God's dwelling which is situated in the higher worlds. The material universe is situated in the lowest Sephira of the Tree of Sephira, called Malkut, which is at the bottom of all created cosmoses. The divine world is situated above the all created metaphysical cosmoses, above the Tree of Sephira, in Ain-Sof. The divine world is not just some world amongst the stars, but a space beyond the material world and also above all metaphysical cosmoses. From here the Heavenly Creator gazes at the worlds that He had created. Try to imagine this divine cosmos!

Chapter 11. The Absolute, Creator of all Worlds

'Our Heavenly Creator,' the mentor continued, looking thoughtfully at the smooth surface of the lake, 'is present in each of His creations, in the entire manifested universe, even though most people do not know Him. He is the essence of each manifested object though we cannot recognize this in our usual state of consciousness.

He created man in such a way that none of the achievements and successes of everyday life will satisfy his soul: neither richness nor glory, romantic love or a happy family life. We will be satisfied only when we have complete unity with the God who created us and installed in us divine capacities. Consciously or unconsciously, man will always strive to reach the divine worlds of the Absolute. Man is born to live with his spirit in the entire universe, and he will never be satisfied with his earthly lot. If we realize that true happiness is to live in unity with the Lord our God, then we will begin to look for a rapid spiritual evolution and thus we will turn to Kriya Yoga.

Each human soul, being a part of the whole, needs a connection with the Creator of all the worlds, in order to become a soul of value and to become perfect. No human soul can be perfect without the support of our heavenly Father. The Absolute is a living, mysterious substance which cannot be comprehended, but with which one can merge. The Absolute is the mysterious source of grace, of the highest love, of an unspeakable bliss and of an incomprehensible form of superconsciousness. He is the mysterious source of life for all living beings, the centre of all the manifested worlds. He is to be found in all his creations, though He dwells beyond the borders of the manifested world and often reveals Himself to pure souls. The Absolute is an incomprehensible mystery; He responds to the prayers of the saints and He helps the innocent souls because they are close to Him. The more egoistic the soul, the more it is separated from other people and the more it is separated from its Creator, as He is also the collective soul of the entire humanity. It is impossible to come closer to the Absolute, by looking for Him in the outside world, but it is possible to see Him when you immerse yourself in the depth of your soul. The human soul is infinite, and it lives in infinity, it is not of this world. Man cannot find perfection until he or she becomes united with the mysterious source of all that lives. Our world can find perfection only if it becomes united with the divine world. When our consciousness merges with the cosmic consciousness of the Creator of the universe and our heart merges with His cosmic love, we will find the Heavenly Kingdom. And only then will we find the true happiness and bliss that we are looking for in our incarnation. Longing for the inner perfection which is hidden in us, points like the needle of a compass. The Heavenly Creator dwells secretly in the depth of our heart and one of the quickest ways of coming closer to the Heavenly Creator and obtaining perfection is the practice of Kriya.

Chapter 12. The Meaning of Suffering

'Can the great Absolute free incarnated humanity from suffering,' asked Kasyan timidly, 'so that we are able to live happily and joyfully?'
'The Heavenly Creator,' answered Alexey, 'does not see it as His task to create a 'paradise on earth' for us. He tries to remind incarnated humanity that earth is just a temporary shelter.
All humanity should eventually embark on the Path of spiritual development and return to the higher worlds, to our spiritual homeland, to our Heavenly Father.'

'Why doesn't He bring all people back into the Heavenly Kingdom Himself'? asked Kasyan.

'Man should reach the heavenly Kingdom by his own efforts and with God's help, and re-unite with God. If man were to arrive in the Heavenly Kingdom as he is now, he will create a secular life there once more, full of diversions and entertainment, making the Heavenly Kingdom a common world, vulnerable to the power of maya, or illusion.

'God's creation is based on the unity and the struggle of opposites,' Alexey continued, 'good and evil alternate like day and night. Human beings are in their essence spiritual beings, made up of divine light, and their bodies are given to them temporarily, so that they can incarnate in the manifested universe. Life on earth is actually an enormously complicated game, like chess, meant to prompt people to grow spiritually and to overcome the illusion of material life. Then human beings will be able to return to their spiritual homeland. However, as the pleasures of life become a kind of glue, our souls become firmly bound to our physical body and we forget our principal task: to return to the Heavenly Kingdom. Only long lasting suffering and failures remind man of a higher purpose to life: to use all our life power for the sake of returning to the bosom of our Heavenly Father. The pain that man feels during his incarnation on earth prompts him to seek God and the Heavenly Kingdom. Just like the prodigal son, who was hungry and could not even manage to elicit swine's fodder, and who only then decided to return to his father, like him man is prompted by suffering to search for something deeper than just money and enjoyment - the Path of spiritual growth.

Human beings are children of light, born from the love of our Creator and each of them has a sparkle of eternal life. But they will never wake from their comfortable dream of material life if there is no suffering and horror of death which forces them to search for spiritual awakening. How cruel this explanation might seem to you,' the mentor concluded, 'it goes hand in hand with the traditional belief that death is the best adviser. Only a few are capable of the great heroic deed of voluntary renouncement of earthly enjoyment, and seek the source of eternal life. Man needs to be prompted from time to time as to the necessity of reaching for his spiritual homeland in the form of bodily suffering and approaching death. Only then will he fasten his eyes on heaven and will stop identifying with his physical body and will wish to return to the bosom of the great Absolute. Only death can force the prodigal son to wake up from the dream of maya and ponder his spiritual nature. If we study attentively what is going on around us, we can see that most of humanity cannot be prompted even by death to search for spiritual wealth. And now we must return home. You have to practise the knowledge that you have received from me, otherwise it will become a useless burden.'

CHAPTER 13. MEETING WITH A CONFEDERATE SEEKER ON THE PATH TO THE ABSOLUTE

After a few days Kasyan said goodbye to his mother and Alexey and returned to Kishinev. A new academic year had started and Kasyan discovered that when he immersed himself in mathematical studies, he did not think about the Path to the Absolute, and only his meditations helped him to remember the purpose of his incarnation. When he returned home after lectures, he would lock himself in his cell and would meditate for four hours. He concentrated on his third eye and practised other techniques that his mentor had given him. Then his soul would come alive and the meaning of life would become clear again and he felt the inspiration coming from the world behind the curtain. Sometimes he ate his lunch at the university canteen. A tall, ascetic man who sat at his table alone, drew his attention. 'Judging from his introverted look,' Kasyan thought, 'I can assume that he also meditates. But to ask him might be tricky, he might report to the dean, and then he will throw me out of the university!'

On one of these days, after he had paid for his lunch, Kaysan went up to the table of the man.

'Would you mind if I join you?' he asked.

'No,' answered the man dryly, 'have a seat.'

'I can assume,' Kasyan said cautiously, sipping at his soup, 'that you practice meditation.'

'Like all the beings who are endowed with reason, I have to meditate often,' answered the man, 'as the word 'meditate' means 'to think deeply.' As I am a postgraduate of biology, I have to meditate even more often than a student.'

'I mean,' Kasyan said, who was not disappointed by the man's ironical answer, 'meditation like they practise in India.'

'Why are you so interested in the subject?' the man asked.

'I want to know more about meditation,' Kasyan said, 'and you look like a person who could be practising something like that. By the way, my name is Kasyan.'

'Gregory,' said the man. 'I am not involved in anything like that.'

'I'm sure you are,' thought Kasyan, 'your face immediately livened up!'

They continued their lunch in silence. When they had finished, the man said to Kasyan suddenly.

'I have become interested in the subject you mentioned. If you have books about 'Hindu meditation', then I would gladly look at a couple of them.'

'I bought one of those books recently,' Kasyan said. 'I could show it to you tomorrow.'

'That would be interesting,' said the man. 'Till tomorrow then.'

The next day, after lunch, Kasyan showed Gregory a book by Shivananda 'Meditation and Life' that he had bound himself. Gregory turned over a dozen pages in a nonchalant way and remarked, 'an interesting book.' Then he took out of his portfolio 'Meditation and Life', which looked almost the same as Kasyan's self-made book, only more worn.

'I have studied this book for several years,' he said and gave an odd smile.

Gradually Kasyan and Gregory became friends and sometimes they meditated together. Kasyan was happy that there was at least one person in Kishinev with whom he could discuss the subtleties and problems of meditation. Then the winter came and after Kasyan passed his winter examinations, he went to the Caucusus. He missed living in Kishinev in the clear atmosphere of the mountains.

Chapter 14. Slowing down the Breath with the help of Prayer

'I concentrated every day on the image of the spiritual sun and on the idea that I am an eternal spirit,' said Kasyan to Alexey when they met again. 'I have also been concentrating on the third eye, as the Hindu guru described, but I feel I should take another step forward. Could you show me a new technique on a higher level?'

'You should learn to slow your breathing with the help of prayer, then you will be able to experience higher degrees of contemplation in prayer. This practice will help you to pull your life energy away from your body, and to immerse yourself in the depth of your soul in a correct way. Our five senses: sound, taste, sight, touch and smell, can function, that is receive information from outside, only if they possess life energy. Life energy can be compared to an electric current. If there is electric current, then there is light in our house and all the electrical apparatuses can function, and we can stay in contact with the outside world. The same is true of the human body: if it has life energy then all the organs of perception function, we move, communicate with others, work, eat and feel content. But if our life energy is taken from our body, or if it is limited, then it stiffens like a wax puppet and we cannot eat or drink, or communicate. We find ourselves in a sort of coma, and the amount of life energy is only enough to let the heart and hearing function. We are made up of two parts as the Christian ascetics used to say: the outer man – the body, and the inner man – the soul. When life energy is pulled away from the body, the outer man falls asleep and the inner man wakes up. This is not the end of life as it continues on another plane. If the life energy is pulled away deliberately from the body, due to special spiritual exercises, then the inner man can enter into a state of spiritual contemplation, or as Christian ascetics called it: 'subtle vision'.

If a practitioner in such a state prays intensely, 'Lord, have mercy on me', he or she can immerse even deeper in themselves and discover their shining spirits - formless spiritual beings with an individual consciousness. Imagine yourself as a formless spiritual being, and, if you want to enter the astral cosmos you must 'put on' an astral body! In the same way, if you want to incarnate in the material cosmos, you should enter the womb of an earthly woman.

The prayer 'Lord, have mercy on me', in combination with slow breathing, will open a passage for you into the divine world. This exercise will help you pull your life energy away from your muscles, your inner organs and the five senses.

Sit down on a chair covered with a woollen blanket or a silk cloth, facing East or North. Straighten your back, stick out your chest and pull in your stomach. Close your eyes, relax your body and concentrate your attention on the point between the eyebrows that is the third eye. Paying close attention to your breath, inhale in 15 seconds, then hold your breath for another 15 seconds. Exhale quickly and hold your breath as long as you can without losing inner comfort. Immediately after inhalation occurs, say the first word of the prayer: 'O Lord' inwardly. During the exhalation, which must also be natural, recite the second part of the prayer inwardly: 'Have mercy on me.'

Continue in this way for 10-30 minutes, then exhale slowly and hold your breath for as long as you can.

In this exercise you should think of yourself as an outside observer, who just notices how breath enters the lungs of your bodily shell and then leaves it. This is usually an unconscious process, but you have to become aware of it.

Gradually your breath and your heartbeat will slow down during this exercise to such an extent that you won't be able to discern them. Breathing binds our soul and body, and if you deliberately slow down your breath, this tie becomes weaker. Gradually you will feel a deep serenity inside yourself, and you will realize that you are a spiritual being, independent of the physical body.

It is best to perform this practice in the morning and in the evening, though you can actually perform it any time of the day or night.

Even in a crowd of people during rush hour in a train, you can still watch your breathing whilst pronouncing inwardly 'O Lord', as you inhale, and 'Have mercy on me', as you exhale. In this way all the time that you wasted can now be used finding contact with our Lord! This practice will help you to get rid of anxious thoughts that will not let go of you.

Do not forget that you should not force withholding your breath, it should happen only in a natural way. If your breath slows down during this exercise, it is a good sign, but still breathe naturally. If breathing stops naturally, keep your mind empty. When breathing resumes, then continue praying 'O Lord, have mercy on me'. Remember that the purpose of this exercise is the natural prolongation of the intervals between inhalation and exhalation, and it is not recommended to keep air in the lungs by contracting the throat muscles.

The slower your breathe, the quicker your earthly personality will calm down and your spiritual essence will awaken; the clearer and more elevated your mind becomes, the closer you will come to the unsolved mystery of yourself and to the link with our Heavenly Creator.

The quicker your breathing, the quicker the heartbeat and the metabolism of your body, and the quicker you will grow old; the quicker useless thoughts will whirl in your head, the more anxious and bad tempered you will become. The stronger your attachment to the material world and the power its charm has over you, the more you will distance yourself from your Creator and the stronger you will merge with matter.

All this will quieten your mind and elevate your consciousness. When you notice the positive results of this prayer, you can use the next one: 'O Lord, Beloved'.'

CHAPTER 15. THE MEANING OF THE SACRED SOUND 'AUM'

'I often read about the various sacred sounds, said Kaysan, could I use the sound 'Aum' when practising this technique?'

'There is a different practice based on the sound 'Aum', said Alexey. 'Every object radiates a certain vibration on the level of atoms and molecules. If you activate your subtle perception you will immediately feel the hardness of the iron vibrations in comparison with the gentle vibrations of wood. Concrete walls in modern houses radiate cold vibrations and people cover such walls with carpets or with wood panels, in order to create a cosy atmosphere and to keep the warmth of the soul in the house. As wood radiates vibrations which feel pleasant to our soul, it is cosier to live in a wooden house. Stones also have hard vibrations, and for this reason it is not pleasant to live in a cave. Flowers on the other had, have subtle vibrations which allow us to immerse ourselves in the world of beauty.'

'Do the planets and stars also radiate vibrations?' asked Kasyan interrupting him.

'Yes, the sun, the moon and the earth have their own unique vibrations. Any planet in the cosmos has its own vibrations. Generally speaking, all the creations of the Heavenly Creator vibrate, and every vibration is actually one of the innumerable nuances of the cosmic sound 'Aum'. This is what the ancient Hindu sage, Rishi, states. They considered 'Aum' a sacred sound, which is the basis of the created universe.'

'What would happen if I meditated on the sound 'Aum'?' Kasyan asked.

'If a practitioner concentrates his attention on this sound and sings it for a long time, then, according to Rishi, he can merge with the consciousness of the great Absolute,' Alexey answered. 'He will see the illusory nature of the manifested world. The space around will loose its firm structure and the practitioner will see that his body and the entire world around him will dissolve in the divine vibration. He will see how the space around vibrates and becomes transparent with atoms and electrons, which, in their turn, are just clots of vibrating energy.'

Chapter 16. Meditation on the sacred Sound 'Aum'

Kasyan got up early and after completing all the practices went to Alexey.

'In order for you to become aware of the fact that everything in our world is based on the sound 'Aum', it is necessary to concentrate your attention on this sound and meditate. I will explain a concentration technique to you, which will allow you to penetrate the mystery of this sound.

Sit down with your legs crossed and with an upright back on a chair, and cover yourself with a woollen blanket. Close your eyes and close your ears safely with your thumbs. Look at the third eye and listen attentively to the sounds in your right ear.'

'Why especially the right ear?' Kasyan asked.

'Because the right ear is more sensitive to astral sounds than the left. First you might hear a sound which resembles the buzzing of a bee, then a sound which resembles the sound of flute, then a sound which might remind you of the sound of a harp. The next sound will resemble the sound of a bell, while the one after will resemble the sound of breakers, and after that you will hear the rumbling of the mysterious sound 'Aum'. Concentrate on this magical, cosmic sound, as this is a link to the divine consciousness. When you hear the sound 'Aum' it means that you have contact with the Heavenly Creator and then you can start praying to Him. In your prayer you can ask the great Absolute to open your heart to divine love. You should also ask Him to help you on your path of spiritual growth. Pray until you receive His answer, divine grace will then come to you, and the mystical flower of love will blossom inside your heart.' With these words the mentor left the room.

Kasyan tried to listen attentively to the sounds in his right ear. Suddenly his attention was caught by a clear buzzing sound in his right ear. Listening to it he felt as if he was entering another world and he felt uneasy. Then the sound changed to something that sounded like a lighter whistling of a flute. The sound of the flute became stronger and sounded like a large church bell, a mysterious rumbling coming from far away. He concentrated on this sound and it was as if the space around him was pronouncing 'A-o-u-m'. Kasyan prayed ardently to the Absolute, asking for help on the spiritual Path and to help open his heart to divine love. After a while Kasyan felt as if a fire was flaring up in his heart. He felt an enormous love and gratefulness to God, and he saw light coming from his chest which seemed to illuminate the entire room. In his heart Kasyan's felt an unspeakable joy and he went to look for Alexey. His mentor was in the kitchen, drinking tea and reading a book. When Kasyan told him about his meditation Alexey became thoughtful for a moment and then said: 'The Absolute dwells beyond His creation and manifests Himself in different ways. He manifests Himself as the Holy Spirit, spiritual joy which is always new; as the sound 'Aum' which pervades the entire visible and invisible cosmoses; as divine love which overfills your heart. Holy people see the energy of the sacred 'Aum' in the third eye, like an opal circle surrounded by blue radiance, out of which there emerges glittering silver rays, encircled by a golden ring. Blue, silver and gold are the colours of the cosmic energy.

In order to penetrate deeper into the sound 'Aum', you should perform the following practice: concentrate on your aura and try to really feel it. Start singing 'Aum' until you feel that the space around you vibrates as well as the earth, houses, trees and people. You will realize that matter is nothing else but vibrating energy. Go on singing 'Aum' until you become completely dissolved in it. This meditation should be performed for not less than one hour a day, and then you will gradually feel that matter consists of the condensed divine energy of light. The sound which comes from the energy during the condensing process, is the sound 'Aum', and if you sing 'Aum' for approximately three to four hours, you will find contact with the Absolute, the Creator. Your consciousness will merge with this sound and will spread itself all over the universe, though you will still preserve your individuality.

In the beginning of this practice, the sound 'Aum' will give you protection and consolation, but when you advance on the Path, you will feel in this sound the pulsating cosmic life, and you will also feel inside yourself the rotation of the earth and other planets, and the light of the distant stars.

CHAPTER 17. THE KRIYA TECHNIQUE

Kasyan went far into the mountains for several days and sang the sound 'Aum' there for hours. When he got tired of singing he sat down with his legs crossed and tried to discern the cosmic 'Aum', although he could not help thinking about the Kriya technique. 'Why should I waste my time on all these auxiliary techniques?' Kasyan thought on the one hand, while on the other hand his other mind sang 'Aum'. 'It would be short-sighted to spend so much time making preparations instead of practising the most important technique which will lead to a merging with the Absolute.'

With this in mind he went to Alexey. 'Please, teach me the practice of Kriya.' Kasyan asked, 'as soon I will have to return to Kishinev.'

'It's a pity that you are in such a hurry,' Alexey answered. 'The creation of favourable circumstances goes very slowly. A disciple should wait humbly for years until his Master finds it appropriate to give him the necessary technique. The disciple will then accept the technique with gratefulness and will practise it diligently, overcoming difficulties. If you practise this technique while unprepared, the consequences could be negative.'

'I don't think I lack persistency,' said Kasyan, 'and I am not afraid to take risks.'

'If you insist, I will explain the basics of Kriya to you,' said Alexey. 'You will be able to practise Kriya in a proper way if you have purified your body, mind and heart and have got rid of negative emotions: scepticism, vanity, pride, depression and laziness. You should learn how to transform your sexual energy, diminish your worldly desires, and keep your mind busy with incessant prayers to God. Ask for the help and support of the great teachers of India. Say inwardly, or aloud, the following prayer: 'O great avatar Babaji, O great teachers Lahiri Mahasaya and Sri Jouksteswar, help me to practise Kriya in a proper way and find the Lord God in myself.'

As far as life style goes: try to eat meat or drink alcohol as seldom as possible. Preferably eat raw vegetables, fruits and nuts, as cooked food does not have much energy in it. Try to be moderate in everything, especially when it comes to sex: not more then once a week, and preferably without orgasm. Perform Kriya not sooner than one hour after a meal. Do not increase the duration of the exercise without consulting me first, and do not teach anyone else this exercise as it could obstruct your own advancement.

'All right, promised Kasyan, 'I will adhere to these conditions.'

'Sit down in the half-lotus posture,' Alexey continued, 'or on a chair, with an upright back. Watch your spine constantly as it has the tendency to bend forward.

You should not lean your back towards any object as your energy will flow away. In order for you to have a good idea of the sensations during this practice, carry out the following procedures: place the edge of your left palm with half-bended fingers on the upper edge of the right hand so that they form a kind of tube. Inhale air through this tube, pronouncing a long sound 'O-o-o-u-u-u' - the air will feel cool. Breathe the air out then, right above the fingers, pronouncing the sound 'I-i-i' at the same time, the air will now feel warm. Both sounds should come from the depth of the throat. Repeat this ten times in order to remember the sensation.

Put your hands together on your knees. Imagine that your spine is a kind of empty tube: one end is the coccyx and the another the third eye. Breathe in, moving at the same time your life energy, your prana, inside the 'tube' from coccyx to the third eye, while pronouncing the sound 'O-OU'.

Still breathing in, move your prana forward through the bridge of the nose to the point a distance of a couple of centimetres in front of the bridge of your nose, and then bring it back, making a U-turn and moving your prana through the point right above the third eye, back into your head. Breathing out, move your prana downwards along the rear of the 'tube' of your spine, back to the coccyx while pronouncing the sound 'I' at the same time. The inhalation is accompanied by a sensation of coolness inside the spinal 'tube', while the exhalation is accompanied by a sensation of warmth along the rear of the spinal 'tube'. The cool energy has a light blue colour, while the warm energy has a rosy colour. The inhalations and exhalations last 10-15 seconds; thus one cycle of Kriya breath lasts 20-30 seconds. At the beginning you can exercise for half an hour in the morning and in the evening, which is equal to 120 Kriya breaths a day.

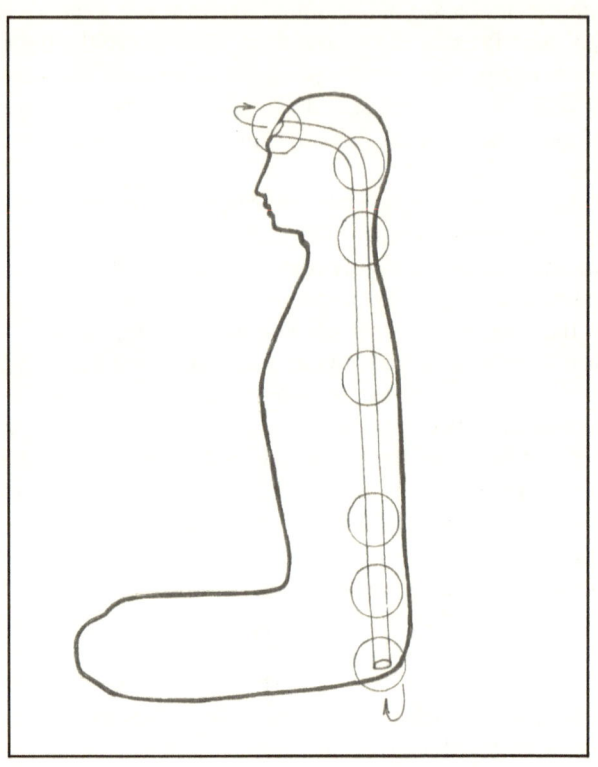

Illustration 4. Circulation of energy during Kriya breathing

'What makes prana move up and down along the spine? Is it just breathing?' asked Kasyan.
'The driving force is our will power,' answered Alexey, 'and breathing also helps in this respect. Normally our life energy, that is prana, circulates around our nervous system and maintains the activity of our organism. The moving prana makes our spine a kind of magnet, which draws all our life energy from the muscles, the inner organs and the five senses. When this happens we are not aware of the outer world, but come into a state of spiritual

contemplation. In such a state our prayer to Lord God becomes ten times more effective.

A joyful, cool and refreshing sensation on the entire trajectory from the coccyx to the third eye during inhalation, is a sign that you are performing the 'spiritual breath', as I call it, in a correct way.

Do not boast about your Kriya achievements in front of your relatives, friends and acquaintances, who are not themselves engaged in this practice!

Chapter 18. Auxiliary Exercises

When you have finished the Kriya exercises you should perform two auxiliary exercises which will help to release the life energy stuck in the muscles and in the vertebra, and will allow it to flow into the third eye. It also helps to prepare the spine for the accumulation of life energy, and the transformation of the spine into a mysterious magnet, which opens a passage for us into the higher worlds. The best way to exercise this is to sit on the blanket spread on the floor, or on a solid bed.

-Bend your left leg so that you can sit on your left foot. Your left heel should touch your anus. Bend your right leg and pull it towards your chest and place your hands and fingers on your knee. The spine should of course remain upright. Breathe in and move the prana upwards, exactly as it is done in Kriya breathing. Hold your breath, bow your head and press your chin to your chest while stretching your right leg forward, still keeping it lying on the floor. With both hands hold the big right toe, and pull it towards yourself, holding your breath for six seconds. Straighten your back, bending your right leg again and pressing your knee to your chest, exhale exactly as it is done in the Kriya technique.

-Repeat this exercise sitting on the right leg while bending and stretching the left one.

-Straighten your back and pull both knees to your chest and perform a Kriya inhalation. Stretch both legs forward and grab your big left toe with your right hand, and the big right toe with your left hand, and pull them toward yourself holding your breath for six seconds. Then straighten your back and perform a Kriya exhalation.

Repeat the whole sequence two more times.

If you perform this technique before exercising the Kriya technique, then your body will be better prepared and practising will be smoother.

The second auxiliary exercise is meant to open the spiritual eye.'

'What does the 'spiritual eye' mean?' Kasyan asked. I have never come across the term yet.'

'Spiritual eye, third eye, inner eye – these are terms which signify one and the same thing: a most subtle part of our mind which is capable of contemplating spiritual reality. Before exercising this technique you should pronounce the following prayer:

'Heavenly Father, let me contemplate with my spiritual eye Your wisdom, let me become aware of Your divine consciousness.

O Heavenly Father, purify my spiritual eye and reveal Yourself to me through it. Let my consciousness follow the dove of light, the Holy Spirit, which descended from heaven into our Lord Jesus Christ.'

When your spiritual eye has opened you will see with it a light blue five-pointed star. The five rays are the manifestations of the five elements: ether, air, fire, water and earth. This small star is actually the door to cosmic consciousness, and the golden radiance around it is cosmic energy. The ancient sage, Rishi, stated that our physical body is nothing else but a materialization of the spiritual energy which our spiritual eye perceives. The purpose of both auxiliary exercises is to open the spiritual eye, and when your spiritual eye opens you should try to pass through the small blue star, which I have just told you about, as if through a door, and then you will come into the sphere of spiritual light. The second auxiliary exercise should be performed three times, directly after the first one.

Christ said: 'Your eye is the lamp of your body, and therefore if your eye is pure then your body will be light' (Matt. 6:-22, Luc. 11:-34). So for this reason it is very important to open and purify your spiritual, or third eye.

Sit in the usual position. Close your ears with your thumbs, and at the same time place your index fingers on the outer corners of your eyes, pressing the eyeballs slightly. The middle finger should be placed next to the nostrils, the ring fingers at the end of the upper lip, and the pinky at the end of the under lip. Make a Kriya inhalation and hold your breath for about 12-25 seconds. Concentrate on the point between your eyebrows and knit your eyebrows tightly. With your index fingers make slight, cautious motions over the eyeballs, pressing them slightly. At the same time press the other fingers, closing your ears, nose and mouth tightly. Then loosen your fingers and make a Kriya exhalation. Repeat this twice.

If you will perform this exercise every day, you will gradually notice a certain tension in the area of your third eye, and you will be able to see a white astral light. If you continue doing these two exercises you will then see a whirling blue light, which comes from the white and blue astral whirlwind. If you continue then you will see a small blue star which signifies that your spiritual eye has opened. At this point try, without delay, to penetrate through this star into another world. Don't be afraid, this is a natural process. Our physical eyes are meant for the perception of the physical world, while our spiritual eye is meant to penetrate the kingdom of the great Absolute, the eternal kingdom of the Holy Spirit, filled with bliss. When you go through the spiritual eye you will need to pass the three gates.'

'What do these gates look like?' enquired Kaysan.

'They all look the same: a white star in the centre of a blue circle, around which an aureole of golden light shines.

However, you will arrive at these gates only if you have practised long enough.

The golden radiance is the manifestation of the cosmic energy from which the world is created. The blue circle is in fact a blue tunnel, and at the end a white star shines which is a mysterious passage into the astral world.'

'What will happen to me when I have passed through them?' Kasyan asked.

'After passing through the first gate you will surpass the limitations of the physical body as you will leave the material universe, and you will enter the astral universe in which you can live in your astral body.

After passing through the blue tunnel and the white star of the second gate, you will find contact with the cosmic, divine consciousness. After merging with the consciousness of the Creator you will find the entire manifested universe inside yourself, wherein you can observe the distant star constellations and the rotating planets.

After passing through the blue tunnel and the white star of the third gate, you will leave behind the manifested worlds, both physical and astral, and will enter the spiritual worlds, the kingdom of the Holy Spirit.'

'How can I realize this?' asked Kasyan enthusiastically. 'Are there methods to achieve this?'

'It is impossible to penetrate into the worlds that you perceive through your spiritual eye if you do not learn to slow down your breathing to such an extent that your body will become as immobile as a statue, and your heartbeat almost indiscernible. As I told you, this can be achieved if you pull all your life energy away from your body into your chakras. And this can be done either by using Kriya breathing, or by the technique whereby you observe your breathing, while saying the prayer 'O Lord, have mercy on me.' Then you will realize through your own experience, that the entire manifested world exists only due to the glory of God, and you will be able to contemplate His glory through your spiritual eye.'

'Could you describe the signs which would indicate that I have come closer to such a state?' Kasyan asked.

'When your life energy starts leaving your physical body, as the result of your diligent practice, you will experience it as a gentle flow of energy from every part of your body towards your chakras. Your eyes will spontaneously look in the direction of your third eye. At the point between your eyebrows you will feel alternating sensations of coolness and warmth. If you close your ears you will hear the sounds 'Aum' in your spine which will gradually spread all over your body. You will see with your third eye a white astral light which will become more and more intensive. When your breathing almost stops, then a dark blue passage to another world will appear before your spiritual eye. When looking at the world through physical eyes, man perceives himself as something separated from life. But looking at the world through his third eye, man sees his unity with the omnipresent Spirit, because behind the third eye lies the higher consciousness of man. As he penetrates the higher reality, which is perceived through the third eye, man reunites with the life-giving God, and immerses himself in the infinity of the spiritual world.

If man can unite the intuition of his heart with his third eye, then man will be able to see the future, the present and the past in all parts of the universe clearly, as all the events in the universe are registered in the Akasha-chronicles, which are accessible to us, when our heart and third eye are opened and purified.

That was it, for the time being,' concluded Alexey suddenly. 'I have told you enough to enable you can take the next step forward in your practice.'

'But I still have so many questions,' protested Kasyan.

'Write them all down and ask me the next time we see each other,' said Alexey. 'Moreover, I will lend you the book entitled 'Autobiography of a Yogi', written by Yogananda, who was one of the disciples of Sri Yukteswar, in which he describes in detail the life of the great teachers of Kriya, and you will find that this book answers many of your questions.'

CHAPTER 19. ACHIEVEMENTS ON THE PATH OF KRIYA

Kasyan returned home and read Yogananda's book within a week. 'It is clear,' he thought, 'that I have to find contact with one of the great teachers of Kriya. Only then can I practise successfully, though it would of course be preferable to find contact with Babaji himself. Kasyan blew up the portrait of Babaji that he found in Yogananda's book, with the help of a beamer, and made a large pen drawing on a piece of oil cloth. He hung the drawing on the wall of his cell, and next to it a small copy of the photo of Sri Yukteswar, that he had also found in the Yogananda's book. Kaysan was attracted to Babaji by his feeling of spiritual might, while the image of Sri Yukteswar spoke directly to Kasyan's heart.

Kaysan's studies at the university were becoming more intensive and he discovered that after many hours of study his soul had virtually no energy for spiritual practices. To combat this, he would go to his cell immediately after coming home, and would spend a number of hours there practising Kriya breathing, and afterwards he would concentrate on the third eye and simultaneously on Babaji's image. After a month of intensive exercises Babaji still did not respond, though the photo of Sri Yukteswar, on the contrary, sometimes looked very lively! While Kasyan practiced Kriya diligently, Sri Yukteswar's eyes looked at him encouragingly, and when Kasyan started thinking of the beautiful women that he had met during the day, Yukteswar looked at him in an estranged manner and Kasyan felt so hurt that he would banish all these seductive thoughts and would concentrate on his third eye once more.

Kasyan thought: 'Babaji is so far away he will not pay any attention to my meditations, while I feel that there is contact between Sri Yukteswar and myself. Sri Yukteswar was photographed exactly at the moment when he was in a state of Samadhi, and if I concentrate on his image long enough, perhaps I will be able to enter into this state as well.' Kasyan placed a photo of Sri Yukteswar in the centre of the wall and an image of Babaji next to it. The contact with Sri Yukteswar became stronger and even the image of Babaji radiated approvingly, as if Babaji was confirming that Kasyan had taken the right decision. After another month had passed by, Kasyan discovered something else interesting. After a long Kriya practice, Kasyan stood up abruptly and stretched himself, his spine straightened and a strong stream of energy rushed from the muladhara chakra to the sahasrara, and in an instant Kaysan had left his body. His spirit flew freely and joyfully in an invisible, infinite space, and when he returned once more to his body lying on the floor, his head hurt because of a large lump caused by a fall. Kasyan bought a hard hat the next day and put it on before he stood up and stretched himself after the meditation! When he strained his muscles his energy flew powerfully upwards and he left his body through the top of his head and he entered the world of shining silver ether. When he got back into his body which was lying on the floor again and he was glad that he had taken precautions. Kasyan continued his exercises concentrating on the image of Sri Yukteswar, and started to feel contact with him as a sort of warm, thin thread which connected his heart to the heart of Sri Yukteswar, and calmness and purposefulness was transported to him along this thread through the Kriya exercises.

After half a year had passed, Kasyan paid a visit to his favourite bookshop in search of books on programming, and while he was thumbing through one of the books, a middle-aged man with a long and untidy beard came up to him. He had an oil cloth bag in his right hand, the contents of which was covered with a newspaper. 'A beggar,' Kasyan frowned, 'he wants money from me, most certainly.' He took a couple of coins out of his pocket and held them ready to dispose of quickly when the beggar held out his cupped hand. The man however just smiled, and said: 'My name is Edward. I sell books, privately, and I have often seen you in this shop. I have a problem and I hope we can help each other. The point is, that according to Soviet law, private business is a crime and for this reason I have problems with the storing of my book stocks. I live in Odessa and I want to make a deal with you. If you keep a couple of dozen books in your apartment, then you may stay here, that is if you would like to have a holiday by the sea? Also, I will let you have one free copy of each title.

'What kind of books do you sell?' Kasyan asked.

'Various books,' answered Edward, 'ranging from fiction and detectives to classic authors. I also have books that would be interesting to you,' he added.

'And what kind of books am I interested in?' Kasyan asked smiling.

'Books like this one,' said Edward, taking out a book from his bag which had the 'samizdat'[2] appearance, so well known to Kasyan, but this time of a more professional quality. Kasyan looked around suspiciously and took the book. The name of the author, Carlos Castaneda was unknown to him, but the title of the book, 'The Path of Knowledge of the Yaki Indians', rang a bell immediately.

'You may have this book for a week, even if you decline my proposal,' said Edward, doing his best to make it sound careless.

'He is very cautious and he has disguised himself perfectly,' thought Kasyan.

'Do you know more people interested in these kinds of books?' he asked Edward.

'Approximately half my clients,' answered Edward briskly.

This was a decisive moment for Kasyan and they exchanged addresses and telephone numbers, and Edward promised Kasyan to bring his books in a weeks time, plus the sequel of the knowledge of the Yaki.

The door bell buzzed in Kasyan's flat on Saturday morning, and when Kasyan opened the door he saw Edward wearing

the same shabby clothes that he had on in the bookshop. Next to him, on his right hand side, stood a huge old brown suitcase, similar to those in use before World War II, and on his left hand side a large military knapsack. Kasyan helped him to carry it inside and was surprised at its heaviness. 'Edward is a cunning fellow!' he thought. 'He looks puny, but meanwhile he can carry such an enormous weight!' Edward glanced curiously at Kasyan's living room, the photographs of the spiritual teachers, and went up to the bookshelves.
'Do you know these people in the photos?' Kasyan asked him.
'I've set up my business due to them,' Edward answered. 'When I was young I was inspired by the idea of spiritual growth, and I spent thousands of roubles buying books on the subject. I studied the teachings of almost all the important Hindu gurus and European spiritual teachers, but I was not better off. I remained exactly the same as I was before, only I was poorer! My wife left me, my friends lost any interest in me as I was always busy with esoteric books or reading them, and I was also dismissed from my work. I decided to sell all my books and win back at least a bit of my money. I turned to my former friends and acquaintances and offered my books cautiously to them. None of them, however, or any of their acquaintances were interested in spiritual development or in spiritual books. As I was an economist by profession I thought: 'I have a product which is not in demand, and so I must create a circle of clients who will be interested in esoteric matters, and then at least I will have clients who might be interested in buying my books.' I became acquainted with young people in the bookshops, and now and then, when it was appropriate, I would mention that I had books to solve any problem. At first they were sceptical, but I learned to talk about spiritual books so ardently that people started to buy them. Gradually a large circle of friends and acquaintances was built up, to whom I supplied esoteric literature. I became acquainted, at least superficially, with all the modern and

old spiritual movements, and I can recognise, at least by name, all the popular spiritual teachers. However, I do not believe that any of their teachings helped me.

When I started to sell fiction as well, my business grew, and I always had at least a thousand roubles cash in my pocket!' While saying this Edward put his hand into his jacket and pulled out a thick bundle of banknotes. He twisted it for a while in front of Kasyan before hiding it once more inside his jacket.

'You have chosen the wrong path,' Kasyan said. 'It's impossible to achieve anything on the spiritual path just by reading books. It would be too easy just to learn couple of books by heart and then think you can enjoy contact with the Absolute! If you meditate then you will understand what its all about. I learned everything I know through meditation.'

'In that case', said Edward, 'you are the first person I have met who understands what meditation is. But we will have to look into that later. Here is the continuation of Castaneda's diaries.' With these words he took the book, entitled 'The separate Reality' from his bag, and handed it to Kasyan, who subsequently hid Edward's books in his wardrobe and immediately dived into Castaneda's story!

Kasyan practised the Kriya breathing every day and, in addition, concentrated on the photo of Sri Yukteswar for an hour daily, asking him questions inwardly, and he duly received answers. Kasyan thought about Don Juan, the Indian magician quite often, and woke up early one bright Spring morning, to see right in front of him, the astral body of an old man with grey hair and a beard, with only the upper part of his body in view. Kasyan was horrified and panic stricken and waved his arms in an effort to drive the visitor away. The figure started to dissolve quickly in the air, and he became less afraid when he saw clearly that it was Sri Yukteswar's face, so familiar to him due to his concentration exercises. ' Oh teacher,' Kasyan pleaded, 'I have been waiting for this meeting for so long! Do not go away, forgive me my reaction, I was jut panic stricken!'

Yukteswar's eyes looked friendly, but his body looked as though it was dissolving, and suddenly disappeared completely. After Kasyan returned home after his lectures, he sat down to meditate and turned his thoughts to Sri Yukteswar and recited the following words: 'I beseech your forgiveness, oh great teacher. I could not bear your presence in the astral body. Please do not leave me and continue to guide me!' He kept repeating this request until he felt that his heart had become peaceful again.

Edward visited him fortnightly, bringing new books and removing stock, each time giving Kasyan a couple of books on various esoteric topics. Kasyan was pleased that his esoteric library was growing and he planned to start studying alchemy and arcanology, and when Kasyan visited Edward in Odessa, he introduced him to his friends and clients, who were also interested in spiritual matters. Kasyan found that the mystics of Odessa enjoyed talking about spirituality more than practising it, and they especially enjoyed parties!

Kasyan successfully passed his summer exams at the university and went to the Caucusus, to visit his mother and his mentor. He arrived at Teberda early in the morning and his mother was happy to see him again, and her eyes were loving and warm. Kasyan ate breakfast with her and then went to Alexey, breathing the fresh mountain air deeply and enjoying the view of the ridges, covered with snow which surrounded the valley.

CHAPTER 20. WAKING OF THE KUNDALINI, OR SNAKE POWER

When Kasyan had finished telling the story of his meditations, his contact with Sri Yukteshwar and Yukteswar's astral appearance, Alexey said: 'It's hard for me to admit that you have advanced further on the Path than I have - you are forty years younger! But I am not your teacher, I can just help you to take your first steps on the Path. To complete my task I will tell you about the technique of waking kundalini, so that you can reach perfection, but first I must warn you of the dangers.'

'I am not afraid,' Kasyan remarked.

'This is a special kind of danger, which is actually part of your own nature,' Alexey said, nodding his head. 'You enter the astral world and experience various subtle states so easily, that you could be inclined to forget the purpose for which you exercise these techniques. You should always remember that you practice Kriya breathing only for the sake of finding God in the shortest possible time. If you always remember your purpose then you will advance on the right Path. But if you forget, even while practising, then you will stray from the Path. The mechanical, automatic performing of Kriya breathing just for the sake of experiencing a supernatural phenomenon, will not lead you to enlightenment. This technique is given as an aid in your search for God. If you forget our Heavenly Creator, you could easily fall into the cold, Lucifer like current, as it is sometimes called.'

'What does that mean?' asked Kasyan guardedly.

'It means that you will feel superior to other people, and you will see others as just a means of achieving your personal goals. Your heart will freeze like ice, and will not be able to feel the divine, subtle and warm vibrations. You should always be careful of yourself, especially when you start waking up kundalini. As the Hindu sages state, kundalini sleeps, coiled in the coccyx. Like a snake, this power is venomous and dangerous, but it also possesses wisdom and strength which can help man to reach the spiritual heavens. Not everybody is able to tame the snake, and likewise not everybody is able to control kundalini, and only a sage can use the power of kundalini to reach the divine state of consciousness.

The power which is confined in the coccyx, has a passage to our sexual centre, which is called the 'dangerous gate'. It is called 'dangerous' because all our accumulated subtle energy can flow away with sexual energy. When this power flows downwards, it seduces a man and a woman into having sexual intercourse, as the feeling of enjoyment with orgasm, is caused by the flowing of this power out of the coccyx. When God created Adam and Eve He gave them complete freedom of manifestation, with the exception of sexual enjoyment. He told Adam and Eve that if they surrendered to sexual pleasure, they would be banished from paradise, meaning that divine consciousness would be extinct in their souls. Those who can make kundalini rise to the brain become enlightened, and those who use this power for enjoyment, fall into an even deeper dream of maya, and become even more susceptible to world hypnosis.

You can see from the representations of the priests and pharaoh's of ancient Egypt, that there is an image of a cobra's head which appears to emerge from the third eye. The meaning of this symbol is that control of kundalini has been obtained, and its power has been directed to the medulla oblongata, and in doing so they are able to reach a divine state of consciousness. It is possible to wake up kundalini with the help of Kriya breathing, but you should always remember what the ancient Hindu sages have said: if you obtain full control over the mysterious snake power you will find God inside you. But if you are defeated by it, then you will be enslaved by it for the rest of your life, and you will suffer without any positive outcome. Death will destroy your body and darkness will take hold of your soul, and you will rush purposelessly through hellish worlds as a homeless spirit, tortured by your passions and remorse.'

'I will try not to forget your words,' said Kasyan. 'But practically speaking how can I wake kundalini?'

'I would like to remind you first of the rishi statement: as long as kundalini sleeps, man's life energy is consumed by the physical body, and man is attached to the physical world. When kundalini has awakened, life energy flows back to its source. It is pulled from the body to the plexuses, and then flows into the chakras. Usually a man or woman's chakras are in an inactive state. When kundalini flows upwards along the channel of the spine, the chakras become filled with life energy and they open up. When the anahata chakra opens up, the practitioner feels the presence of the heavenly Creator in his heart. When the brain becomes filled with life energy, then the sahasrara chakra opens up and the practitioner's consciousness merges with the boundless ocean of the consciousness of the Absolute. This state is called 'samadhi' in the Hindu tradition .

Chapter 21. The Technique of waking up Kundalini

Sit as you do for Kriya practice. Roll your tongue backwards and press the end to the uvula. Focus your half-closed eyes at the point between your eyebrows , keeping a quiet facial expression at the same time. Strain the muscles in the perineum until you feel that the life energy flows upwards along the spine, concentrate on the muladhara chakra and chant 'Aum' once inwardly. While inhaling, move your life energy from the coccyx along the channel of the spine, to the point between your eyebrows and pronounce 'Aum' inwardly, passing each chakra. When you have reached the point between your eyebrows, start exhaling, moving your life energy at the same time downwards along the channel of the spine, once again pronouncing 'Aum' as you pass each chakra. Continue this exercise until you feel the vibration of life energy in your spine. Every half-hour, after raising your life energy to the third eye, hold your breath and rotate your head anti-clockwise ten times. Pronounce 'O Lord have mercy on me' at the same time. When you stop rotating you might feel that your life energy has been drawn away from your body and your spine, and fills your sahasrara chakra. If your breathing stops at this moment, you could experience the state of super consciousness. However, the technique of waking up kundalini should only be performed under the supervision of an experienced Master. When kundalini reaches the sahasrara charka, it will open up and you will experience the state of samadhi. In this state man finds unity with the

Absolute, the heavenly Creator, with His Son and with His Holy Spirit.

'Could you tell me more about the state of samadhi?' Kasyan asked his mentor.

Chapter 22. Samadhi

'Samadhi is the highest possible state according to the Hindu sages,' said Alexey. 'This is the state of perfect union with Spirit as man's soul dissolves in the highest Spirit. This is called the first level of samadhi. On the second level of Samadhi, man feels one with the entire universe. Man is then able to perceive the entirety of life, not only on earth, but also on the other planets of our universe. He actually perceives the whole universe as his body, and the pulsation of the cosmic energy as his own breath. He will feel the heartbeat of all the people on the planet, and feel that his mind is one with the minds of all people. He can feel what every person feels, as if he has merged and has become one with them. Only his bodily shell separates him from other people, but his soul has become one with all human souls.

He is also able to perceive the slightest motions and changes of the entire universe, from the spinning of an atom to the rotation of galaxies. He sees that matter is just coagulated energy, he sees how the divine light becomes matter, and how matter becomes divine light again. He sees how the divine Spirit penetrates the entire universe, and how every single drop of individual self merges with the ocean of the divine Spirit. He sees that life and death are just one of the illusions of cosmic maya, the world hypnosis. The different levels of merging with the divine consciousness correspond to the different levels of bliss and wisdom, when the soul merges with the Spirit only for a certain limited period of time. He realizes that by merging fully with the Absolute, he becomes a source of eternal joy and bliss.

If you practice Kriya breathing diligently, you will also be able to experience such elevated inner states, beyond the manifested cosmos, while still in this incarnation. Kriya breathing is very different from similar techniques from other traditions, which demand strict celibacy. This is important in modern times, as it is rather difficult to protect ourselves from the sea of hypnotic information which destroys our intention to preserve celibacy. The Master of Kriya does not put such rigorous demands on disciples nowadays, he just asks for a certain moderateness in sexual behaviour, which is sometimes hard to define today, and every practitioner has his or her own estimate of what moderation means. My advice, however, is that the less you give in to the lure of the lower chakras the better.

The human soul is enveloped by the tree shells which keep it imprisoned in the manifested worlds. The first and coarsest shell is our physical body; the second is our astral body, created from the coagulated energy of the Great Astral; while the third is the causal body.

The human soul can free itself from the limitations of these three shells if man is willing to make super efforts, and is willing to practise Kriya regularly under the guidance and protection of a spiritual Master. The reading of esoteric literature and philosophical treatises only will not help. Judging from your story, Sri Yukteswar is such a Master to you. By practising Kriya you will be able to open your seven chakras, your seven seals, and reunite with divine consciousness. It is a Path full of hardship because most people have forgotten about their divine origin, and no matter who tries to remind them, they just respond with a grin.

Your discipleship with me has come to an end, as I have passed on to you all the knowledge I have. In order for you to advance further, you need the guidance of your true Master, but the question is, will you be able to find him?'

'From my twenty-second year,' Kasyan answered, 'I knew intuitively that when I turn thirty I will meet my true

Master. My life will change completely then and I will have to move to Moscow.'

'Why Moscow?' Alexey asked.

'I do not know,' Kasyan answered, 'this is what I learned during one of my meditations.'

'Moscow is a dangerous place,' said Alexey, 'you'd better be prepared then for this meeting so that you will be able to stand it.'

Chapter 23. The State of Super-consciousness

Kasyan spent some time in Teberda and then returned to Kishinev. He went on practising Kriya breathing and the special technique to wake up kundalini.

Once in the night, during the practice of Kriya, his breathing felt as if it had stopped and his body stiffened and felt like a wax statue, and his consciousness spread over the infinity of the universe. Kasyan could still see the walls of his cell, but at the same time he saw innumerable stars inside himself. It was such a strange feeling that he did not understand what exactly was going on. Kasyan's consciousness then left his immobile body and ascended into space, where there is no manifested universe or life that is comprehensible to us. It was an infinite space and Kasyan realized that he was the radiance of the Absolute, a spirit, a formless light which had consciousness, but which did not have any bodily restrictions. Although he felt that his individuality had dissolved into the flow of God's grace, still he felt present. Kasyan realized that what he was feeling was his boundless highest self and not his bodily shell with all its problems. It was an immense joy, to fly all over this vast space beyond the manifested universe, with the help of just a thought. He was everything and, at the same time, he was nothing. He was a bodiless, infinite spirit, blowing in an infinite space above all the worlds, all the cosmoses. He had no limits, no boundaries, but, at the same time, he was an individual possessing reason. All his being was filled with bliss from this merging with divine consciousness. Somewhere, far below, he saw the planet earth, like a small blue ball and he felt his body which, he realized, had nothing to do with his true essence.

This state of super consciousness lasted for about an hour, and then some power made his body breath normally again and Kasyan returned to his usual state. He knew that he had become aware of a great mystery, but on the other hand, he was still the same person, with all his shortcomings. It was as if God had taken him into His invisible expanse and had shown him who he really was, bringing him finally back once more into the manifested cosmos. Kasyan felt torn as he was extremely happy that he had entered into the divine world and that it was the home of his soul, but on the other hand he was sad, because he realized how long the Path is to this world, and how many obstacles he would need to overcome in order to stay in this state of consciousness forever.

Chapter 24. A Gift from the Goddess Sarasvati

Every day, while performing his exercises, Kaysan expected his kundalini to wake up again so that he could once more experience that extraordinary state. He managed to get out of his body more than once, but he could not find that elevated unity with the divine consciousness. In search of a clue Kasyan started to reread 'The Autobiography of a Yogi' and the chapter entitled 'The Heart of the Statue' drew his attention. Yogananda described his visit to the temple of the goddess Kali in Dakshineshwar. This was the temple where the spiritual teacher Paramhansa Sri Ramakrishna worshiped the light aspect of Kali. Yogananda sat for five hours in the lotus posture in this temple, praying to Kali and asking her to show her light aspect to him. He was almost desperate after many fruitless attempts, when suddenly Kali responded to his prayers. It seemed as if the temple has become several times bigger and its wide gate opened and the huge figure of Kali appeared. The space around the statue started to vibrate and the statue came alive. She nodded her head and smiled at Yogananda affably. Yogananda then described his state of super consciousness in which he could perceive every single detail of the world around him, even many miles away from him. Kasyan was inspired by this vision of Yogananda and decided to exercise Kriya, praying at the same time to the beautiful goddess Sarasvati, the spouse of god Brahma and the patroness of science and art, as a large portrait of her hung on the wall of Kasyan's living room. After sometime his breathing became almost unnoticeable, and he felt as if the gate to another world had opened in his chest. Suddenly he saw the beautiful Sarasvati dancing a mystical dance of eternity, before the Creator of the Universe surrounded by the whirlwinds of space. This amazing vision lasted for about halfanhour, and Kasyan's soul enjoyed the wave of bliss coming from Sarasvati.

His last similar experience was when he was about twenty-five, when he realized that worldly life had kept him in its grip, while Kriya had not given him any concrete results. Kasyan continued with his regular practices despite everything; he turned thirty, but still life continued without any change and there were no sign of his true Master - his life seemed hopeless with regard to his spiritual growth. Deep in the night, however, he received a clear message from Sri Yukteswar telling him that if he went to Odessa, he would find what he had been waiting for for such a long time. Hesitatingly Kasyan journeyed to Odessa and finally met his Master, whose name was 'G'.

'For many years,' said G, 'you have sat and meditated, but in fact you don't know yourself or life. These methods can help you grow, only if you become a completely different person and transform yourself radically. Such a transformation can take place only if you leave behind your old life and follow me. Our travels will become your schooling, and at the same time you will help me to bring the spiritual message to the people.'

'What do I have to do?' asked Kasyan mistrustfully.

'You must help me to build an ethereal school,' answered G, 'where those who are ready can follow the Path of Ascension. You will be able to ascend to higher spheres only if you help others to ascend. Only then will the heavenly hierarchies help you to ascend into the higher worlds.'

'Will you help my friends as well, those who also trying to follow the spiritual path?' asked Kasyan. 'It is not an easy task as most of them are stuck with books about the spiritual path, and will have difficulty recognizing you as a spiritual Master. They either believe the books only, or become completely disillusioned with the books and consequently do not believe in the existence of the spiritual Path at all!'

'I will give all of them the opportunity of stepping on the Path,' answered G. 'However, you should not depend on their decisions.'

Neither Gregory nor Edward, or any of Kasyan's friends or acquaintances recognised what he saw in G, and they had no intention of changing their lives. Only a recent acquaintance of Kaysan, an eccentric lover of esotericism, called Gouri, also recognized G as his Master, to Kasyan's great astonishment. Kasyan and Gouri spent nineteen years of their lives travelling through many cities and towns in the Soviet Union and Europe with Master G, helping him to build as he used to call it, 'alchemical stills'. Kasyan became another person, as many spiritual mysteries and secrets were revealed to him, and he helped hundreds of people detach themselves from earthly problems and aspire to God, but the feeling of heaviness in his soul was sometimes unbearable and the spiritual worlds seemed to become more and more inaccessible to him.

Chapter 25. A Message from the higher Worlds

Kasyan had a constant headache for about a week, day and night, which was annoying. He decided to check his blood pressure, which turned out to be abnormally high, and he visited the doctor for the first time in fifteen years. 'Your blood pressure is so high, I do not understand how you are still alive,' he said thoughtfully, checking the meter, and he called an ambulance without paying any attention to Kasyan's protests. As a result of innumerable hospital tests, Kasyan gradually realized that his health was completely ruined. 'Without a miracle I will die soon,' he thought, 'And what about the enlightenment that G promised?'

He phoned G and asked him to visit him in the hospital, and he arrived the next day accompanied by a neophyte, called Stargazer, who had an expression of fear in his eyes. 'From what I have heard from the doctors,' Kasyan said to G, 'I am about to pass into another world; and I am still far from enlightenment.'

'If you think about the reason why you were submitted to hospital,' answered G, 'then you will be able to recover. You have been helping me, and you have received many spiritual insights. However, you were so carried away by your success that you did not listen to my warnings and you let your emotions govern you. This was the reason why the guardians of the threshold of the School, transferred you from the spiritual front line, to the hospital at the back, so that you could come to your senses. If you realise your faults, then you will be able to return to a forward position, and you will be able to help me, as before, to further spread the prophesy of the School. But if you give in to your depression and continue to justify yourself, then I will have to postpone our meeting to some other incarnation in the future.'

'How should I amend my mistakes?' exclaimed Kasyan. 'And what are these mistakes? I did everything I could to help you achieve your purpose!'

'You never listened to my words which explain that the priority is not the achievement of outer purposes,' said G, 'but the inner work on yourself, the purification and perfection of your soul. Start working on this now, and believe me, your situation is not as hopeless as you think. Just start working on yourself.'

'But how?!' Kasyan cried out. 'It's true, you always told me that I should 'work on myself'. But you never told me exactly how I should do it!'

'Just meditate on it,' G said. 'I assure you that you will be able to find a way out.'

G and Stargazer left, and Kasyan felt drowsy and when he was out of his body, he found himself in an unfriendly, desert-like place, standing in the large crowd of people. A kind of concentration camp surrounded by barbed wire. 'I'm dead,' Kasyan thought, 'so this is the way it's all arranged!' Every morning the gate of the camp opened and a select group of thousands of people walked on a broad straight road towards an enormous woman, who stood far away towering above the horizon. She had a sword in her right hand and scales in her left hand. Looking at her, Kasyan, to his surprise, noticed that when someone walked under the scales, the dishes moved. If the dish from which a black smoke was rising was heavier, then a woman would wave her sword and the person would disappear in the black cloud. The camp was always full, however, as new souls that had left their bodies kept on arriving.

Kasyan could remember his entire earthly life and only his consciousness was slightly dimmed, and he found himself in the group being guided to the gate. At this point Kasyan suddenly re-entered his body on the hospital bed. 'This was a message from the higher worlds,' he thought. 'They have shown me that death is close, but, at the last moment I was allowed to return to the earth. This probably means that I have been given another last chance to amend what I have done wrong. G always told me: 'Stop wasting your precious energy by feeding the dragon in your soul. Do not use my energy to increase negativity. Do not indulge your primitive, uncultivated instincts, stop expressing negative emotions; remember yourself' G, however, never told me how I could realize this and I knew I would have to solve his riddles in order to survive.'

After another week Kasyan was dismissed from the hospital. 'We cannot help you anymore,' said the doctor. 'Your blood pressure is a time bomb, and we do not know how to defuse it.'

Kasyan returned home and immediately felt the presence of death. 'It is as if it wants to remind me about 'work on myself,' thought Kasyan, and he left his apartment so as not to feel its horrifying presence. He decided to go to the centre of the city, just to distract himself from these heavy thoughts. Suddenly he felt the cold breath of death at the back of his head and he suppressed an impulsive wish to run across the road amongst the rushing cars. Sitting in the bus later, he was horrified to see a young man crossing the street in the same manner as he had intended only a short while ago. A large black car hit the man at enormous speed, and rushed on without stopping. The man flew into the air and fell like a sack of sand on the asphalt. 'This is another sign from death,' decided Kasyan. 'I have to do something, otherwise I will be the next victim.' He got off the bus at the next stop and went home by foot. The atmosphere in his apartment was quiet once more and he spread a woollen blanket on the floor and sat down with his legs crossed for the first time in many years, and immersed himself completely in meditation. 'If death comes to me,' he thought, 'it means that I have neither bodily energy nor a soul. The first thing I have to do is restore my energy, then I will have time to figure out how to work on myself.'

Kasyan inspected his big esoteric library that was still growing. A book by Taisha Abelar called 'Magical Crossing' and her technique of reconsideration drew his attention. 'This seems to be the core of the problem,' thought Kasyan. 'I thought that I was giving the energy of the School to others, to inspire them to grow spiritually, but it has turned out that I have also used up all my own energy!'

Kasyan made a list of all his former girlfriends, relatives, friends and enemies, and began to to exercise the breathing technique of Toltecs, described by Taisha. After a week of daily practice of reconsideration for approximately four hours a day, he felt that death was not following him so closely anymore, and was kept at bay.

Kasyan was encouraged by his first success and learned several series of Toltec movements for life energy manipulation, and exercised them every day.

His energy was coming back and his health was getting better little by little, though he was still depressed and could not enjoy the world around him; the trees, the sun and the sky, and he thought: 'The light has abandoned my soul, that is why I feel so depressed. The technique of reconsideration works and my energy is returning, but this technique is not flawless, and it is very improbable that the wasted and polluted energy from the past can be purified by just 'breathing out negative emotions' as stated. In addition, by slightly rocking the head it is possible to break the ethereal ties with someone only on the level of sex and instinct. The soul- and spiritual ties, however, remain untouched, and my energy still flows away, feeding the people from my past, with whom I have nothing in common now. The Toltecs teaching is rather naïve, and their strongest point is magic and astral manipulations, but they know almost nothing about the higher worlds of light from which I was excommunicated, and with which I want to find contact again.' Kasyan could not find the answer to this question, and the feeling of heaviness in his soul started to grow again. Looking for a way out, he turned once more to his library and glanced through various esoteric books, full of different advice and techniques, but his soul did not respond to them. He came to the conclusion that all these books were about building an interesting life, while he was constantly feeling the presence of his death. In this strange light, all the esoteric treatises that he used to be so fond of, seemed to be superficial. He found a small book, presented to him by Gouri, who was serving as a psalm-reader in a small parish church. The book was entitled 'The Secrets of Life after Death.' Amongst other things Kasyan had read about the posthumous ordeals of the soul of a nun called Theodora, and suddenly a spark of hope flared up in him. He sat down to meditate and thought: 'The only path I always wanted to avoid in all my exercises and practices, was the Christian path. Because for some reason it always seemed to me that the Christian path would not suit me. But what will happen if I confess to the priest all that I have already reconsidered? It might help me to purify my soul from all these soul- and spiritual ties.'

Kasyan went to the evening service and confessed his sins to the priest: his pride, and a liaison of his a year ago, and he received communion. He realized that the bad memories of this short relationship which he could not forget by reconsideration, had disappeared.

'I should combine the reconsideration technique with repentance and confession,' Kasyan decided. 'Repentance frees my soul from all subtle soul and spiritual ties with worldly people. My soul has become completely entangled in them, and this is what makes me depressed. As G's assistant I had to inspire other people to follow the spiritual Path, for which I was rewarded with many spiritual insights. However, I have sinned and this has been the result of what G defined as: 'Letting the passions rule'. He was right, there is a way out, and if I repent all my sins my soul will become radiant again.'

Kasyan went to church every day and used the lists that he had made for reconsideration to recall his sins and he confessed them, one by one, every day, to the priest. 'You are a proud man,' the priest said to Kasyan's after his turn to confess. 'You extol yourself in front of other people and therefore you condemn them. God does not appreciate the proud, and He does not come to you. And you are suffering because God's love is not in you.' On another occasion the priest said to Kasyan: 'Learn to forgive other people and God will also forgive you your sins.' Kasyan prayed to the Mother of God to rid him from his jealousy of Irina, an old love of his. They had broken long ago, but Kasyan still felt the break like an open wound and could not forget all the angry, horrible words they had said to each other, and even worse were their negative feelings towards each other, a mixture of hatred and fatal attraction that hurt him the most. Suddenly, as he stood gazing at the icon, a prayer came into his head, as a gift from above. 'O most holy Mother of God, as I stand before you I ask Irina to forgive me all my insults that I caused by word, deed and thought; known and unknown to me.

O most holy Mother of God, standing before you, I forgive Irina all her insults to me that she caused by word, deed and thought, known and unknown to me.

Let me not condemn her, but let God judge me.' Immediately after this prayer Kasyan felt that his soul had become lighter, as if part of the black deposits deep inside had evaporated by the invisible fire of his prayer. 'On one hand, my soul is purified by confession,' Kasyan though with a warm feeling of joy in his heart. 'On the other hand, now I can perform this myself, with the help of the Mother of God. Now the whole process will go much quicker.'

Kasyan phoned Gouri and asked him to send him some more books about Christianity. Gouri sent him, amongst other books, the biography of the last Staretz[3] of the Optina Cloister, the priest and the monk, Father Josef, who was the favourite disciple and spiritual heir of Staretz Ambrosias. Kasyan read it through and was inspired by the Staretz Josef teachings of self-reproachment. He spend many hours after that standing in the church in front of icons repenting his disobedience when he neglected G's instructions and gave in to his passions. He felt that after each act of repentance his soul was becoming lighter and more joyful, and his blood pressure had also become normal.

Kasyan spent many years working on the purification of his soul, and the results exceeded all his expectations. He returned to G, full of strength, and G was seemingly not surprised. Kasyan felt that his soul was filled with the mystical wind of the School and her wings had been spread again. When G invited him to accompany him on his trip to Amsterdam, Kasyan immediately accepted.

Chapter 26. The Suggestions of Sri Yukteswar

During the first night in Amsterdam, Kasyan heard the clear voice of Sri Yukteswar in his dream: 'You must begin a new life. You have partly purified your soul, but inwardly you have not reached a high enough level in order to assist G sufficiently.' Kasyan woke up and took a large photo of Sri Yukteswar from his bag that he had taken with him, and he felt an ethereal impulse coming from the teacher. He looked at Kasyan reproachfully as if to say: 'The time has come to leave all your daily concerns behind you, and to start practising Kriya Yoga seriously. At first you lacked G's fiery impulse, but now, after many years of studying with him, your practice will be successful. Begin without delay!' The silent words of Yukteswar made such an impression on Kasyan that he performed the Kriya exercises the next morning.
The words of Yukteswar indeed seemed to ring true, because Kasyan could successfully practise the purifying breathing technique of Kriya. Kasyan kept himself busy for a couple of hours every day doing Kriya exercises. However, after a month of intensive work, he found that he hadn't come any closer to the Absolute. Gazing into Sri Yukteswar's eyes, Kasyan pleaded with him to reveal to him, even for just an instant, the emanations of the Absolute Origin of all the Origins. 'I have followed the spiritual Path for so many years,' Kasyan said grieving , 'but I have not yet found contact with the Absolute.' Once more he received a silent answer from Yukteswar: 'Master G initiated you into a mysterious meditation, which provides contact with the Absolute Source of all Sources, but you have forgotten it all.' ' I have not forgotten ,' Kasyan answered Sri Yukteswar. 'I just thought that I had lost contact with our heavenly

Father because sometimes I do not practise the technique of reconsideration correctly.' 'Don't give up,' Sri Yukteswar said, 'and try to restore this contact through ardent prayer.' Kasyan remembered what Master G had once said to him: 'I think the Absolute Creator of the universe is an abstract entity to you, and you seem to think that you can find contact with Him through opening one or more chakras of yours. The sooner you rid yourself of this delusion the better. There is a direct Path to God: you should purify your body, mind and heart and you should pray incessantly to Him in order to establish a personal relationship with Him. This is the quickest, but at the same time, the most difficult Path. The great danger is that if you defile your body, and if you pollute your heart with impure desires and your mind with impure thoughts, your personal relationship with God will be broken. This is because He is always pure and filled with love, and His thoughts are always clear, and He appears to us as a spiritual, everlasting, radiant, crystal clear sun. He will not communicate with someone whose soul is impure.'

Kasyan went on practising Kriya while praying to God at the same time, and during the practice his breathing became almost unnoticeable and his life power was drawn away from his organs of perception to the chakras in his spine. Kasyan lost the sensation of his body, and his mind stopped its endless turmoil. At the same time Kasyan started to pray ardently to our heavenly Father, pleading with Him to appear even for an instance, to stop hiding Himself behind the invisible curtain of maya. After a short while Kasyan felt light in the area of his spiritual heart. The light became brighter and stronger, until it filled his heart with an incredible radiance. And it was then that Kasyan began to realize the mistake he had made during his meditations, and that the many years of work on himself had seemingly been useless. He realized that he had actually been searching not for contact with the Divine Absolute, but that he merely wanted to experience a state of higher consciousness, he wanted to feel ecstasy;

to feel the infinity of the soul and her eternal nature. In fact what he had wanted to experience was a long-lasting ecstatic state of super consciousness, the same feeling that he had experienced after intensive meditations when he was twenty two years old. And that, he began to realize, was his biggest mistake. The great Absolute, the Creator of the universe and all living beings was always near, behind a most subtle and invisible barrier. Only in a deep inner silence is it possible to find contact with the Absolute, and only under the condition that you will truly long to find Him, like someone lost in the desert longs for a drink of water. It is also necessary to have the help of a teacher who already has such a connection with the Absolute, because it's impossible to find the right direction and to penetrate the barrier of the mind and of the heart alone. Today, however, Kasyan was extremely lucky because he had managed to establish a personal connection with the Absolute. He continued to practise Kriya, reciting inwardly the sacred name 'Absolute' with each inhalation and exhalation, and the light inside him shone even brighter with an incredible power.

Then Kasyan concentrated his attention on the image of Sri Yukteswar, whose eyes suddenly started to radiate the invisible light of the Heavenly Creator that had made Kasyan's heart tremble. He realized that the Great Absolute manifests Himself in the universe that He created in an innumerable number of ways: He is infinite, unfathomable and indefinable, and it's just our earthly mind that tries to set limitations and laws for His manifestations. The Absolute penetrates the whole of the manifested universe, but He hides Himself from us behind the thin curtain of the phenomenal world. Though this curtain is as thin as the cobweb, it's not easy to penetrate.

The Absolute can manifest Himself as a radiant heavenly light, as the Holy Spirit the Consoler, as the love of the Divine Mother, through the holy people and spiritual teachers. He is spread invisibly in the whole of nature, He reveals Himself through the highest love and in an infinite number of other forms that are not yet known to us. However, notwithstanding the variety of His manifestations, we cannot recognize, understand and cognize Him, unless we find Him within our hearts and establish a most subtle contact with Him there.

Kasyan began to understand that the Absolute is not just a philosophical abstraction. He really is the living Creator of the phenomenal world and man can talk to Him in the silence of man's heart. It all depends on how far you open yourself to Him, and how deeply you feel the blessing of His presence. Kasyan then realized that he should establish a solid personal relationship with the Absolute.

After his meditation Kasyan went for a walk in a small wood in Losinoostrovski . Though the spring sun was shining above, the ground was still covered with half a metre of deep snow. Kasyan wandered in the forest and his heart rejoiced , for he was immersed in a mysterious conversation with the Creator Himself.

It wasn't a state of samadhi, in which Kasyan could see in his inner world the whole of the manifested universe with all the glittering and rotating galaxies spreading into infinity. He managed to find a most subtle contact with the Absolute, and this almost unnoticeable closeness to Him gave Kasyan an incredible feeling of bliss.

The world around Kasyan did not care about his feelings, as he walked in the melting snow, while having at the same time an incessant conversation with the Creator of all the worlds.

It seemed to Kasyan that the Absolute was an abstract and unattainable entity which he would never be able to get to know. Kasyan had been defining the enlightenment that he was striving for so zealously most of his life, as: the 'opening of the higher chakras'; the 'sensation of infinity', as an 'experience of the greatness of the universe', as the 'state of superconsciousness' or as 'feeling the heavenly light inside'. Kasyan realized that most importantly he should become aware of the living nature of the Absolute and establish a personal relationship with Him, as fine as a cobweb which is carried by the wind in autumn. 'It's the most important discovery of my life,' Kasyan thought, 'now I know how to penetrate through the shroud of the visible world.'

He returned home, sat down in a meditative posture and immersed himself in his inner world, continuing at the same time to contemplate his invisible connection with the Absolute. Kasyan concentrated his attention on the right side of his chest, which is, according to the spiritual masters, the dwelling place of our spiritual heart. The left side is the place of the earthly heart, which is the receptacle of experience and the emotions of our persona and its problems. The earthly heart or, the emotional centre, according to Gurdjieff's terminology, is the arena of struggle and the clashes of the different selves of man of which he has a hundred. Man argues and fantasizes day and night, basing his thoughts on the same question: 'What might happen, if...'. There is no end to this stream of imaginary events and this is the reason why our consciousness is darkened with endless thoughts. Kasyan discovered that the spiritual heart was the door to the Absolute Source of all Sources. When Kasyan concentrated on his relationship with Him, the world around became unspeakably beautiful and unrecognisable, and he felt love towards all human beings. He realized that the whole of humanity is an integral living organism, all parts of which are indissolubly tied to each other. He also realized that the heavenly Creator is the collective soul, not only of the whole of humanity, but also of all living beings. 'This was exactly the reason for Bodhisattva's vow', thought Kasyan, 'to incarnate until the last living creature is saved. However, this kind of integrity was revealed to me only when I found contact with our Heavenly Creator. It all depends on my perception: if I perceive the world through my emotional centre, then I see only the shortcomings and contradictions of the world. But when my spiritual heart opens I am carried away from the lowest level of perception to the highest, where true unity is revealed to me. I observe that the paradoxical and unsolvable duality has disappeared, and the ancient riddle of the Sphinx, the riddle of the hidden and mysterious nature of man is revealed to me. I perceive the whole of the phenomenal world and millions of events simultaneously. At the same time I penetrate a secret door in my spiritual heart and enter the other world, the world of divine bliss, and I see a thin curtain between the two worlds inside me, which is always there, dividing the visible and the invisible. Both worlds are then equally real to me, the only difference being that the external world has a beginning and an end, while the spiritual world is eternal because the Almighty Creator dwells therein. At his point I don't have questions anymore, because all the answers are have been found: they are traced by the mighty hands of the Ruler of Providence.

But how can I explain to those who have not yet penetrated the mysterious curtain, and which words should I use?' Kasyan felt as though he was on the edge of two worlds: the earthly and the spiritual, in the depth of his spiritual heart. On the one side he saw the world of incarnated human beings, while on the another he saw the spiritual world. From the manifested world the spiritual worlds don't exist, because they are beyond a material and shallow perception, and when Kasyan concentrated his attention on the spiritual world, he could clearly see the illusory nature of an earthly existence. Kasyan also realized that the spiritual world is logical and understandable only to those who enter an invisible door and penetrate the mysterious curtain within their hearts.

After meditation Kasyan went for a walk. The streets were flooded with sunlight and the birds were singing. Kasyan, however, was still enjoying, deep within himself, the mysterious conversation with the invisible Creator of all that exists. Kasyan felt the fragrance of the heavenly worlds pouring upon him from the metaphysical summits. An unspeakable inspiration came to him and his soul was filled with radiant light. His heart thawed and lost its primeval cold and radiated love to all living beings. As far as Kasyan could remember, he never allowed himself to smile at passers-by, but now, with his heart open, a smile appeared without even trying. He was astonished by the change in himself and his usual haughty grimace had disappeared.

'Is this really you?' Kasyan asked himself. The passers-by rushed along, immersed in their own problems like fish in large aquariums. They didn't notice the miraculous change in Kasyan, as if they were stuck to the surface of their personalities. 'The people around don't feel that I am present in two worlds at the same time,' Kasyan thought. 'Obviously they are too busy with their worries and problems and don't have time for the mysterious revelations of the Creator of heaven and earth.'

The next morning Kasyan went to church. He bought candles and put them before the icons of Saint Sergi of Radonezh, Saint Seraphim of Sarov, and Our Lord Jesus Christ. Then he went up to his favourite icon of Our Lady of The Orb.

When he entered the church for the first time many years ago, he looked for an icon of Our Lady that would answer his prayers. He had passed this unremarkable icon many times, but didn't have the inclination to pray there because it seemed to him that the icon did not really radiate God's blessing. However, once during the morning liturgy, the crowd of parishioners pushed him right up towards the icon, and so he was forced to pray and repent before the image of the Mother of God. Suddenly the image of Our Lady came alive and looked unspeakably beautiful. Kasyan stiffened in amazement, looking at this wonder of transformation, and from that time on he stood close to the icon during the whole service, and admired the divine beauty of Our Lady as he repented his sins before Her. He was glad that the other parishioners didn't notice the miraculous quality of this icon, and so there was always space before it. Kasyan lit a candle and gazed once more at the holy image which was very dear to his heart, with a feeling of great veneration. The eyes of Our Lady came alive and filled with light as she fastened Her eyes on Kasyan. Kasyan prayed until his soul was filled with heavenly light. He then bowed to the ground and went home. He decided to return home not through the crowed street , but by following a small path winding through the forest. Kasyan walked on the thawing snow as he prayed, feeling at the same joy, because Our Lady's countenance was still in his heart. He felt bliss and an incredible support from the heavens. He was unspeakably happy at the thought that Our Lady had given him an opportunity to enjoy Her holy presence.

When Kasyan returned home, the image of Our Lady dimmed as he had so many chores to do, and his soul sank once more into the dusk of everyday life'.

'I see,' reasoned Kasyan, 'that because of my imperfection I can stand the contact with the divine worlds for a short while only: my soul is not purified yet from earthly attachments.

Kasyan got up early the next day and practised Kriya again and his spine filled with a subtle energy and started vibrating, and his chakras opened gradually. Within a couple of minutes he could feel the spiritual impulse coming from G, and the deeper Kasyan immersed himself in this impulse, the clearer he felt that there was something immeasurably mysterious behind it. The spiritual impulse of his Master filled his soul with a powerful energy that gradually penetrated Kasyan's entire being. Only then did he realize how far he had moved away from the School, as he was dragged into the daily routine. Support of the Master was like a mouthful of cool water in the desert,

and Kasyan immersed himself in the contemplation of this spiritual impulse. After some time he felt support coming from the higher spheres, a stream of power entered his heart and Kasyan knew what he should do.

Every morning Kasyan practised Kriya for several hours, as if he was doing heavy work. The first hour was relatively easy, but then it became more difficult. However, when he managed to reach a sort of contemplation, he did not notice the flow of time. He could then see how his heavy karma was transformed step by step, and when he was confronted with the next inner barrier, it felt unbearable to continue exercising the technique. His legs ached terribly, and his body felt so heavy that he fell asleep instantaneously. When Kasyan woke up, all his inner selves would revolt against the work on himself, against the practice of Kriya.

The importunate flushing of the lavatory in the neighbours flat was as if underlining the presence of the dark trio: uroboros, kundabuffer and jammer: that another world doesn't exist, and that the Absolute is just a beautiful philosophical concept.

At such moments Kasyan recalled the stories of the temptations of the great Russian saints, such as those that Seraphim of Sarov had undergone during his period of seclusion. Demons came to him in the cold nights of winter and told him to leave the Sarov Cloister. More than once they threw the trunks of fallen pines into his cell and tried to scare him off, and the words of Kasyan's Master crossed his mind sometimes during such moments. His Master said that on the left side of Kasyan's body, there lived many proud rebels who fought against any sort of work on oneself, and who deny the Path to God. They would try to push Kasyan off the path, and use any opportunity to achieve this. However, the practising of Kriya gave Kasyan the strength to ward off the revolting groups of his inner selves, and start transforming them. The process of transformation progressed with great difficulty because the dark trio resisted heavily and induced depressive states in Kasyan. They tried to convince him that the work on oneself was just an attempt to escape the problems of life, and that the Kriya practice was nothing but a trap for fools. The dark trio tried to coax Kasyan to lead a materialistic life with its imaginary values and to renounce his quest for God.

Kasyan, however, wasn't impressed, and didn't stop working on himself no matter how hard it was. Kasyan didn't want to die with his soul still darkened, without becoming fully aware of the depth of his Highest Self and without finding God, and for this reason he followed the instructions and advice of his astral teacher, Sri Yukteswar and Master G, with all his strength.

Chapter 27. Praying to the Holy Trinity

Kasyan woke up and discovered with sorrow that after yesterday's attack of the dark trio, his faith in the great Creator of the universe had been burnt to ashes. Even though Kasyan felt that he was materialistic, he still did not succumb to the resistance of his embittered mind, and he started doing the Kriya exercises. Only one thought circled around and around in his empty head: 'I've spent so much time on different spiritual practices, and it was all for nothing: the dark company has destroyed all my achievements in just one evening.'

However, after an hour of practising, he joyfully discovered that all his achievements on the Path were still intact. His kundabuffer had done its best to deceive him as usual, but it had not managed.

While doing the Kriya exercise, Kaysan recited, as he had done the day before, the name 'Absolute', but without any result. After some time his astral teacher prompted him to pronounce the words 'Lord God', and soon his entire spine shone with the white light.

Yesterday it was not clear to him how the three faces of the Holy Trinity of the Christian tradition, correspond to the Absolute of the Hermetic tradition. The notion that the Absolute is the Creator of the universe fitted well into Kasyan's perception, but the notion that God the Father, God the Son and God the Holy Spirit, who are one in the Holy Trinity and are also the Creator of the universe, and equal to the Absolute, was incomprehensible to Kasyan. Today though, Guru Sri Yukteswar prompted him to recite the invocation 'Lord God', and it was like a password to the higher spheres. The invocation 'Absolute' had previously been opening heavens for Kasyan, but today the password by which he could enter the higher dimensions had changed, and Kasyan's soul didn't respond to the word 'Absolute'. By reciting the words 'Lord God' and concentrating on the thought of God the Father, Kasyan managed in a short time, to come closer to the heavens. His breathing almost ceased and his heartbeat became almost unnoticeable. He lost all sensation in his physical body and his consciousness became focused on two points: his medulla oblongata and his heart. He realized that the words 'Lord God' had the same value when praying to the Creator of the universe, as the word 'Absolute'. Kasyan felt that the most subtle energy had filled his sahasrara chakra, and he became aware of the mighty power of God the Father, the Creator of our universe, of His power and His glory.

It wasn't a feeling of inner bliss; feeling the immeasurable power of God was quite a different experience. Kasyan realized that the power of God the Father exceeds anything that the human mind can imagine. God the Father sustains the whole universe with His power; His will supports all the worlds.

'The innermost door to our Creator opens only if there is a sincere desire to meet Him; insincere prayers won't help. Our heavenly Father is not an abstract figure; He is more real than the whole of His creation. Therefore He doesn't respond to insincerity, and only when He sees that the person praying needs this meeting deeply. If there is no desire to meet our heavenly Creator in the depth of one's soul, then no matter how long we pray to Him, He will never reveal Himself,' thought Kasyan.

Kasyan enjoyed a walk in the forest after this realization, and when he returned home he began practising Kriya once more. This time his breathing ceased quite quickly; the door to the higher dimensions opened in the centre of his chest; he felt inspired and a prayer was born in his soul: 'Oh great Creator of the universe, reveal Thy radiant countenance to me.'

Kasyan recited this prayer repeatedly, and the waves of an incredible feeling of happiness surged through his soul. Kasyan realized that when he exchanged his quest for God for a striving to experience the various states of superconsciousness, all the work on himself got stuck. For many years he had spent his energy seeking the higher states of consciousness, and this was a mistake. Instead, he should look for the most subtle contact with God. For if the connection with the Creator of the universe is intact, then the states of superconsciousness will also follow. God answers a persistent knocking at the heavenly door, which is in fact the daily practice of prayer with a pure mind.

CHAPTER 28. PRACTICE IN THE WOODS

The spring sunshine was shining brightly, and Kasyan went into the Losinoostrovski wood to practise Kriya for a while. He wandered for a long time, carrying a folding chair with him, looking for a secluded place with a good atmosphere, until he saw an attractive looking pine tree that stood next to a birch tree, as if embracing it. The ground under the trees had a fresh radiance that felt comfortable to Kasyan. He stepped off the path and walked through the snow that reached his knees. He flattened a small place under the pine tree, installed his chair and, after baring his torso as he used to do when he was young and strolled in his native mountains, he began doing the Kriya exercises. The place filled him immediately with prana and inner peace, and the blinding sun sparkled on the thousands of snow crystals. When Kasyan's chakras were filled with the ethereal energy and started to vibrate, he focused his attention on the centre of his chest and felt an incredible feeling of love in his heart. He stayed in this state for quite a long time, until he remembered the words of Master G: 'You are capable of becoming the man of nucleus, whose function is to inspire and to warm the hearts of all the disciples of the School with the warmth of his heart.' Before it seemed to Kasyan just an exaggeration, and a kind of unnecessary burden that G wanted to impose on him, but now he understood what G meant by this.

Kasyan placed the images of the most significant disciples of the School in his heart, and prayed to God asking Him to give these people strength to follow the Path. At first he felt that their hearts were cold, but he prayed until he felt that the images were warmed by the love which poured from the higher worlds.

The next day Kasyan went to the place of spiritual power once more. He forced his way through the deep snow, sat down under the pine tree and immersed himself in the Kriya practice. The spring sunshine was pleasant, but a northern wind blew which brought with it the cold spirits from afar and these spirits cooled Kasyan's heart and it closed. A heart which is cold, cannot feel the wave of heavenly love - the secret door vanished and Kasyan couldn't immerse himself in the depth of his heart. Being stubborn by nature, he continued practising Kriya, but when he realized that all attempts to open his heart had failed, he returned home, where it became even more clear how his heart had cooled.

He drew out of himself, with the help of reconsideration, the ethereal lines in which the cold spirits had entangled him, and his heart became warm and humane again. He immediately started practising Kriya and within an hour had lost sensation in his physical body; his breathing became slow and his lungs took in just a small amount of air; and his heartbeat was almost unnoticeable. Finally the secret door to his heart opened again and Kasyan could restore contact with the heavenly world, with God, the Creator of heaven and earth. The wonderful feeling of love pouring from heaven had restored the warmth of his heart and filled it. Kasyan tried once more to transmit God's love to his school friends, and felt that the divine warmth consoled their souls, and in return they responded warmly from the depth of their hearts.

Chapter 29. A Prayer to Lord Jesus Christ

The next day Kasyan started the breathing practice of Kriya once more. After a while his chakras vibrated and he went into himself. This time he felt a wave of love from the higher worlds and his soul trembled with happiness. To feel the might and the Glory of God the Father is an experience beyond expression; like the exultation of the soul that feels love flowing from the heart of our Lord Jesus Christ.

Gradually Kasyan established contact with God, with the help of a heart prayer. 'God is love,' said Christ, and Kasyan prayed to God in the language of love. When he moved energy up and down his spine, he pronounced the Jesus prayer: 'Oh Lord Jesus Christ, have mercy on me.' Gradually his spine filled with energy and all his chakras started vibrating. The Lord then answered Kasyan's ardent prayers and he received a strong spiritual impulse which revealed to him many mysteries of the Path. Kasyan then moved on to another prayer: 'Oh Lord Jesus Christ, illuminate me'. His heart became still and silent and he could hear the Lord's answer telling him that he should unite all his spiritual knowledge in one integral teaching and write a book to help Christians searching for salvation, and also telling him how to make use of the ascetical experiences from different traditions and the information of the saints who found God in them. 'I will have to unite all the knowledge,' Kasyan thought, 'that I've found in the School while following the spiritual Path, in a practical teaching which will help the spiritual seeker to prepare his consciousness for the perception of our Lord's message. I will have to combine the techniques to purify karma with Tao techniques, in order to transform sexual energy, with the techniques of Kriya, which will help man to make contact with the divine consciousness and create an integral system of doctrines and practices. However, I should take into consideration the spiritual experiences and admonitions of the Christian holy fathers.'

The message of our Lord inspired Kasyan so much that he was ready to start immediately, and now he knew what he should write, and how to best help believers and support their quest for God.

Chapter 30. A Prayer to Mahavatara Babaji

While still continuing the practice of Kriya, Kasyan began to pray to the Hindu avatara Babaji, until he felt that Babaji had heard his prayer. Kasyan remembered clearly how fifteen years ago, in one of Kasyan's conscious dreams, G entrusted him to bring one of his disciples to Babaji. Kasyan wandered in the Himalaya for a long time, and finally found the cave where Lahiri Mahasaya had met Babaji a long time ago.

Together with G's disciple, Kasyan reached the high steep rock which towered above the river, and suddenly Babaji himself appeared on the top of the rock in all his radiant glory. He was dressed in a white dhoti and stood still while looking intensely at the strangers before him. His copper-reddish hair reached down to his waist and Kasyan gave a gentle push to his fellow-traveller, as if saying that Kasyan's mission had been accomplished, and he should go to Babaji alone. Babaji, however, fastened his eyes on Kasyan as if he was expecting some reaction from him. Kasyan couldn't utter a word, because he thought that he did not need the advice of other teachers, because he had already received instruction from G. 'How strange,' he thought, 'in my youth I pleaded tirelessly with God, asking for a meeting with Babaji, and now, when I finally meet him, I'm not impressed.' And then he read the answer in Babaji's eyes: 'Though you have constantly been at the side of your teacher, you sank and got stuck in your negative karma.' When Kasyan woke up he felt indescribably ashamed of his indifference to the great Babaji. Although it had happened twenty years ago, Kasyan couldn't forget the reproachful look in Babaji's eyes, and it had taken Kasyan ten years of intensive spiritual practising to purify his soul from heavy karma - karma that had been created because he was not willing to work on himself and take the advice of the great teachers.

Kasyan retrieved an oil portrait of Bababji that had been lying around covered with dust, and hung it up again.

While practising Kriya the next day Kasyan started praying to Babaji once more. The invisible door in his spiritual heart opened again and heavenly bliss filled his heart with the most tender love. Kasyan could never have imagined that Babaji would pour such bliss into his heart.

Chapter 31. God's Voice

Kasyan went to church the next day in order to receive Extreme Unction and rid himself of his heavy karma. The church was filled with plump discontented women and querulous old ladies pushing one another and speaking loudly. It was very difficult to concentrate on God with the bustle all around him.

When the service started the parishioners stopped talking, but Kasyan still couldn't find inner silence, though the dark spots of heavy karma in his soul slowly evaporated and his soul felt lighter and lighter.

Kasyan went home and feeling worn out he fell asleep. When he woke up he realised that his ethereal lines had become entangled with all the people at church, and his individuality had just dissolved in the crowd. In order to return to his subtle inner state he had to urgently practise reconsideration, and after taking back his ethereal lines from the chaotic parishioners, Kaysan managed to regain his lost individuality.

He made a note in his mind that God had revealed Himself in a mysterious space, in church, after prayers, from somewhere above, and not in the inner silence of the heart. Kasyan's heart had shut itself off almost completely due to the crowd of people around him. During the liturgy Kasyan noticed how a stream of divine grace descended from the church's dome, into the flock.

While practising Kriya the next day, Kasyan felt once more that his breathing had almost ceased, and the mysterious door in the centre of his chest had opened. Kasyan's soul was filled with gratefulness to the heavenly Creator, and he inwardly recited a prayer of thankfulness. Kasyan's feeling of stillness and bliss was so pure and inspirational, that the emanations of the astral orders felt heavier, because of their karmic burden, while inner conversation with the heavenly Creator, on the contrary, gave only the lightest feeling of joy.

Kasyan asked himself why is it so difficult for man to find contact with our heavenly Creator? But after practising Kriya, and praying to our Lord Jesus Christ at the same time, Kasyan managed to restore the subtle thread of contact with the heavenly Creator, and heard the divine voice which came from the depth of his heart: 'There are three kinds of work that man should accomplish. The first is work for the sake of the life of the body. The second is work for the sake of the salvation of the soul. And the third is work in My name.

The longer you spend in the salvation of your soul, the closer you come to salvation. The more sincerely and diligently man works for the salvation of his soul, the more stable his contact with Me will be, the Creator of all the worlds.

The third kind of work is to wake people from dream of maya and teach them how to do the work of the second kind, the work for the salvation of their souls, for the sake of their spiritual growth. This work is accomplished by spiritual teachers, who have already found their salvation. They come into this world obeying My command, and sacrifice their heavenly life.'

A deep serenity came upon Kasyan's soul, and for the first time in his life, after many years of work on himself, he heard the voice of our Lord inside him, which resembled a mysterious universal bell.

'In our society,' he thought, ' it's considered normal if man works for eight or twelve hours a day for the sake of his bodily needs. For the sake of the salvation of one's soul, on the contrary, a couple of minutes per day is considered to be sufficient. Many think that the second kind of work is just a waste of time. However, to care only for one's bodily shell is a deep delusion. Man doesn't want to realise that he is an immortal soul, who will reap the fruits of his bad deeds after the death of the bodily shell. For in the eyes of our Lord, to work for the sake of the salvation of one's own soul and to care only for the physical body, is a sin, and the majority of people think that if there is a God, then the bringing of all people back into the Kingdom of Heaven is His concern. And if He needs contact with his good-for-nothing children, let Him take care of it Himself. For if He is almighty, why doesn't He remove all the obstacles hindering His contact with his prodigal sons and daughters?

CHAPTER 32. BABAJI MAHAVATARA AND BABAJI FROM HANDAKAR

Kasyan read the book 'The Incomprehensible Babaji', all night long. Many of the disciples stated that he resembled the Babaji whom Yogananda had described in his book 'The Autobiography of a Yogi'. But the more Kasyan grasped their stories, the more obvious it became to him that Yogananda was describing another teacher who didn't at all resemble the great avatara Babaji who brought back Kriya Yoga to the world. . Avatara Babaji was stern and inaccessible, even to his nearest disciples Lahiri Mahasaya and Sri Yukteswar, and only occasionally did Babaji meet those teachers of Kriya who were predestined to play a significant role in widely spreading the teaching of Kriya in the western world . This new Babaji, on the contrary, invited his disciples from all over the world to join in the building of a temple in Handakar, and communicated with them actively, but didn't impart any knowledge of Kriya yoga to them. He suggested that his disciples, use the mantra 'Om Namah Shivaya' which he considered to be the holiest mantra, the meaning of which is, according to him: 'Oh Lord, Let Thy will be fulfilled.' This new Babaji apparently said to a disciple of his, an old lady, that Jesus Christ was one of his dearest disciples! Kasyan knew that the great avatara Babaji would never say such a ridiculous thing, because Babaji is very close to our Lord Jesus Christ and carries out his spiritual mission in full accordance with the Lord's will. 'It's most probably just a coincidence of names,' thought Kasyan, 'which is no wonder, because Babaji in fact means 'respectful father' and is used very often as an address to all spiritual teachers. The teaching of Babaji who was very active in the 70's and 80's, was not about Kriya, but Karma Yoga. His message to his disciples who followed the path of Karma Yoga correctly, was to love their neighbours and to help them in everything they did, and only then would they would reach enlightenment. A group of his most faithful and devoted disciples built a temple dedicated to him, at the foot of the Himalaya, and many of them said that sometimes he induced in them a state of super consciousness.

Kasyan came the conclusion that the behaviour of this young Babaji was in direct opposition to the behaviour of the ancient avatara Babaji. The young Babaji had obviously taken a lot of the karma of his disciples onto himself, and was more like an ordinary person now, contrary to the radiant youth that he was before. His disciples, however, still stated that he had not lost his supernatural abilities. Soon after the temple in Handakar, which was dedicated to him, was built, he became ill and died at the age of thirty six.

Chapter 33. Kasyan's Experiments with the Kriya Technique

In the first days of March, Kasyan learned a modification of the Kriya technique and he prayed to the Holy Spirit during both inhalation and exhalation. Before, when his breathing ceased, Kasyan concentrated on his spiritual heart. A mysterious door then opened in his spiritual heart, and he could communicate with his heavenly Creator. Today, however, when he turned to the Holy Spirit, all his energy concentrated around the area of the third eye. This energy was different compared to the energy that he felt when he was conversing with God. It was a brighter energy, like a concentrated scorching light. It didn't quieten, but on the contrary scorched Kasyan's soul with an invisible fire. The communication with our Lord felt like a gentle and tender wave of grace and mercy, while the energy of the Holy Spirit was fiery, and Kasyan's soul felt as if it was burning.

Day after day Kasyan gathered his experiences of communication with the metaphysical world, enabling his inner being to grow, and he thought that all these mysterious metaphysical achievements had become possible due to the endless practising of Kriya.

The whole night he had felt a spiritual wave, full of grace, coming from the divine Mother, and so the next day he started practising with a prayer to the divine Mother. He prayed to her until he felt that She answered him with a wave of love. Kasyan felt how the power from above guided and controlled his practising.

After a while he heard a new instruction from his astral teacher inside him, telling him to pray during the practising of Kriya, to the most holy Mother of God. Before She had appeared to Kasyan in the outer world, he saw her countenance, full of grace, above the domes of churches that she protected with her invisible protective veil. She often responded to Kasyan with heavenly bliss when he prayed deeply. However, he felt these visions and help coming to him from above, from the spiritual heavens. Now, when he prayed to the most holy Mother of God, Kasyan suddenly felt that She revealed Herself to him from the depths of his heart.

The great Mother of God revealed Herself in all her might, and Kasyan was shocked by the experience. She freed him, only by Her presence, from many inner problems, and Kasyan realized that Her influence is as great and boundless as the influence of the Divine Mother, who is worshipped by the holy in India, and this was to him a completely unexpected discovery! His heart was filled with an indescribable joy and many of the contradictions and dissonances in his soul were happily solved.

When Kasyan woke the next morning, he realized that after a night of sleep he had once more lost the thin thread of contact with our Lord, and he had to restore the contact again.

He immersed himself in his inner world and start practising Kriya, but only after persistent prayer could he find heart contact with the Lord Jesus Christ and only then did his heart find peace. Though Kasyan had everything that life could offer him, without contact with the worlds of our Lord, his soul felt anguish because it couldn't find consolation in the materialistic world. He felt that his incarnation was totally in vain and he couldn't find peace, and there was nothing that could substitute the joy of contact with our heavenly Creator, for that was not a bodily joy, but a spiritual one. God's gentle and beautiful voice came from the depth of Kasyan's soul and brought a deep inner peace.

The next day Kasyan practised Kriya prayers for several hours, this time praying to Saint Seraphim of Sarov at the same time. Gradually an unusual light illuminated Kasyan's soul. Saint Seraphim was very severe to Kasyan at first, but when Kasyan made a decision to renounce many worldly pleasures, Saint Seraphim changed. After hours of practising Kriya, combined with prayers to Saint Seraphim, the light which came from the great Russian saint filled Kasyan's soul. Kasyan was extraordinarily happy because he had moved the great Christian ascetic, and Saint Seraphim had blessed Kasyan by allowing him to serve our Lord Jesus Christ and let him feel the divine light. During this practice Kasyan felt very clearly that he was not his physical body. Today the separation from his body took place on a deeper level and Kasyan could clearly remember his past incarnations. Kasyan regretted that his present incarnation was also coming to an end.

Gradually Kasyan realized that he had fallen into the trap of wanting to receive 'unearthly pleasures'. His striving to experience yet again such states as the sensation of infinity, void, and his attraction to the stars, had taken Kasyan away from his search for God and directed him towards Lucifer. These inner states don't know love and compassion, and the more time Kasyan spent meditating on the void and the infinity of the starry worlds, the more he felt removed from other people and the cooler his heart felt. Kasyan felt perplexed, but when the Master reminded him that he should love other people, Kasyan just became indignant. Only now, after exercising Kriya for a long time, had Kasyan begun to understand Master G's words.

Our heavenly Creator is the collective mind and spirit of the whole of humanity also, and in the depths of their souls they are united with the divine Spirit, and when man finds unity with God, he feels unity with the whole of humanity as well.

And so Kasyan realized that the spiritual seeker shouldn't practise just for the sake of practice itself: practice is just a means of finding God inside your soul.

Kasyan wandered in the forest, which was becoming alive once more after winter, and asked himself where he would go to after he had lost his bodily shell.

He met a few people who passed by and saw that they were completely identified with their bodies and were not aware of the fact that we are all children of the heavenly Father. Kasyan, however, walked beside the white birch and shapely pine trees, observing with his inner eyes the mysterious inner world inside his heart, while with his bodily eyes he observed the outer world, and he found it interesting to stay within the borders of infinity. When he forgot his inner world, a mysterious door behind which the metaphysical depth lies, closed, and he found himself on the other side of the border again, in the outer world, far from the omnipresent Creator of the universe. He then felt unbearably sad, because the outer world couldn't give him what the inner world gave him. The inner world couldn't exist without God as it was God's inalienable part.

Chapter 34. Prayer to our Heavenly Father

The next day, after performing Kriya, Kasyan managed to draw his life energy from his body into his spine and his body stiffened and became motionless. Then he prayed ardently to the heavenly Father:
Oh Lord, reveal Thyself to your child, Thou art my divine Father.
Oh heavenly Father, allow me to return to Thy dwelling, let me cling to Thy throne.
Oh Lord, be with me here as well, in the manifested universe.
Oh Lord, let Thy omnipresent attention dawn upon me.
Oh Lord, reveal Thyself to me in Thy radiant beauty.
Oh Lord, our heavenly Father, don't abandon Thy children, don't deprive them of Thy divine presence.
The great Creator of the universe heard Kasyan's prayers and revealed to him His invisible countenance in the stillness of Kasyan's heart. A feeling of inner bliss seized Kasyan and the light shone inside him. His heart felt a lightness and freedom that he had never before experienced, and he realized that there is nothing more beautiful in the world than the divine countenance of our heavenly Creator. An incredible inspiration came to him and his heart rejoiced contemplating the divine beauty of the heavenly Father. Kasyan was perfectly silent inside and could see the barely perceivable glimmer of the divine worlds, hidden in the depth of his soul. He became fully aware of the fact that the heavenly Creator is truly alive and omnipresent, but He hides His countenance from those who are ignorant and doesn't reveal himself to Pharisees and arrogant people. It's not necessary to study books in order to perceive the

absolute beauty of the heavenly Creator, it's necessary to quieten your mind, to slow down your breathing and then pray to God and ask Him for grace so that He will reveal Himself to you, even for just an instance. The more books we read and the more theories we learn the prouder we will be, and the further away we will be from our Lord. We must only slow down our breathing, stop the motion of our mind, and pray, when the stillness dawns upon us, to our Lord asking Him to reveal to us His mysterious countenance. If we are sincere in our prayer and silent within, He will respond and will reveal Himself to us. And when He reveals Himself to us we will immediately realize how simple it is to contact Him.

The Heavenly Creator conceals His omnipresent countenance behind the finest barrier of the limitation of our consciousness, which resembles a thin web. There is a mysterious door and if we enter it we can meet Him. However, without His help and His consent we will never find this door, even though it's located somewhere inside our soul. This mysterious door is so transparent and fine that our rough consciousness won't remember its location. The door is always behind the barely discernible covers of our delusion.

Oh Lord, do not leave me alone in this perishable world. Do not leave me for long ; help me to contemplate in complete silence Thy unforgettable countenance.

Oh Lord, let me at least sometimes enjoy Thy invisible presence.

Oh Lord, Thy divine countenance always brings new joy. It is more beautiful than all the beauty of the manifested world. It looks lovingly on us eternally from the bottomless depth of Spirit. It is barely noticeable in the lightest blow of wind, in the fragrance of flowers and in the rustle of the grass.

Oh Lord, Thou art bliss, poured out everywhere. Thou art as beautiful as the unfathomable. The wings of the spring breeze carry Thy loving gaze. Thy invisible countenance is concealed in the beauty of the spring flowers, in the petals of roses; I see Thee in the snow-white petals of jasmine. And still, this is not Thee, these are just forms of Thy manifestations.

Oh Lord, Thou art the inspirer of poets, Thy pour out Thyself in the fragrance of flowers in the summer meadows, and still this is not Thee. For Thy mysterious countenance is always concealed behind the barely noticeable barrier in our consciousness.

Chapter 35. Contact with the Absolute through the Third Eye

By concentrating for a long time on the third eye and applying a certain Kriya technique, Kasyan managed to reach a higher level of perception. A shining passage appeared in his third eye, through which a most subtle contact with the Absolute, the Creator of all worlds was established. This contact resembled a gentle breeze that could disappear at any moment, and Kasyan realized that this concentration on his third eye was different. It was necessary, while practising Kriya, to pay attention to the third eye and pray to God at the same time to ask Him not to hide behind the invisible door, but reveal Himself, even for just a moment.

The concentration of the third eye together with constant prayer to our heavenly Father had another positive aspect, besides a gentle and tender communication: Kasyan's heart remained quiet and not polluted by chaotic emotions. 'In this way,' Kasyan thought, 'it's possible to live a normal life and still keep a focused attention on the third eye while continuing a conversation with our heavenly Father, through that fine, almost unnoticeable contact with Him. No one around me,' Kasyan quietly rejoiced inside himself, 'will be able to detect my inner conversation with the heavenly Creator. For the connection is established by the use of such a subtle energy that it is undetectable to most people, and while immersed in deep prayer, I can still seem a common person . On the other hand, when I communicated with the heavenly Creator through my open heart, when in the company of people who were worn out by life, it was a negative experience, and their heavy energy immediately stuck to me like a burr. One can easily feel the hearts of others people during contact with the heavenly Creator, and through my heart I am open and vulnerable.

When my heart opens to the higher worlds,' Kasyan reasoned further, 'I still remain in contact with the rough atmosphere of my environment and the entire 'common' life. In this way I function as a kind of cleaning apparatus which cleans the polluted atmosphere of the city where I live, and this is the reason why the heart channel of my connection with the heavenly Father became polluted once more. However, when I have contact with the heavenly Father through the open third eye, all these problems disappear, and even if I am in the company of materialists, their atmosphere does not poison me!'

For several days Kasyan tried wherever he could, to keep this subtle contact with the heavenly Father. He discovered that what he had guessed was true: The energy of other people couldn't interfere with his meditations and prayers, and he had become as if invisible to them, even to the dark spirits, as if he had disappeared from the radar of their perception, and they left him alone.

Now he could continue his conversation with the heavenly Father, subtle as a cobweb which blows in the wind, and people around him were not aware of it. .

This was the reason why Kasyan had problems with his health. He worked automatically, against his will, like a 'cleaner', and one illness followed another, because Kasyan couldn't put an end to it. None of the psychological methods such as putting an imaginary mirror in front of him, or building up an imaginary concrete wall, or other techniques helped to protect him. Methods which he found in the esoteric treaties didn't really help him either. So he was happy that his problem had finally been solved and his inner world was protected, even during long train rides, as he simply became 'invisible' to them.

The next day Kasyan had to visit many people for business reasons, yet he still he managed to find four hours to practise Kriya. Kasyan thought about the fact that God, besides manifesting love to His children, is also the Creator and ruler of the whole universe. He is the invisible King of the universe who hides Himself behind the multitude of His creations, and establishing contact with Him is the most complicated and elevated task for man.

The Absolute, King of all worlds, possesses an incredible power, with which he rules the entire universe with all its galaxies, innumerable systems, billions of planets and stars, and many of these planets are populated by living beings.

The Absolute is immeasurably stronger than the prince of this world, or Lucifer, or all the dark powers of chaos and madness.

The wisdom of the great Absolute, the Creator of the universe, is immeasurable and manifests itself fully throughout all the worlds created by Him, His supreme consciousness is infinite and contains all and everything that was created by Him.

The Creator of the Universe possesses an unsurpassed will for realization. He is life giving and His perfection exceeds the perfection of His entire creation. Repeat !

The ascetics from all times strove to find contact with the heavenly Creator, and they spent their lives enduring great torment and hardship for the sake of being able to communicate with the Absolute source of all sources. Most often the Creator of the Universe talked to them in the language of divine love, and the holy men and women who reached their goal and established a constant contact with the Absolute, never returned to secular affaires, but immersed themselves forever in the contemplation of God almighty. They forgot the world and lived in seclusion, breaking it only on God's command, in order to show the Path of Enlightenment to the lost ones.

Chapter 36. Meditations on the Images of Mahavatara Babaji and Sri Yukteswar

Kasyan prayed to Mahavatara Babaji for a long time, practising Kriya breathing at the same time. He then entered into a state of superconsciousness and saw that the consciousness of Babaji is inseparably merged with the consciousness of the Creator of the Universe. This vision made it clear to him why Babaji is called 'an incarnation of God on earth'. As Babaji's consciousness is merged inseparably with the heavenly Creator, he constantly co-creates with Him. Babaji is not a separate person, his consciousness is united fully with the consciousness of the heavenly Creator. The more intensely Kasyan prayed to Babaji, the stronger became the spiritual light coming from him. At one point Babaji's light became so strong that Kasyan couldn't stand it; it felt as if the light was scorching him. Kasyan's body flamed from within with an invisible fire, and Kasyan remembered Sri Yukteswar's explanation that the practice of Kriya gradually prepares our body for the perception of the divine energies of light. Their intensity is so great that the soul of an unprepared man can burn out in the radiance of the divine light, and Kasyan realized that he was not yet ready for such an intense 'temperature', and so he prayed to the spiritual teacher Sri Yukteswar while practising Kriya, and his breathing slowed down to such an extent that Sri Yukteswar could induce a state of super consciousness in him. It was, however, a different state: Kasyan didn't feel that bright spiritual light which scorched his soul, but a gentle cordial atmosphere which united him with the Creator of the universe. Kasyan realized clearly that the Absolute is present in every man. He remembered Christ's words: 'Love your neighbour as thyself,' and he could now understand the true meaning of it: every human being is the child of the Absolute and there lives in each of us a particle of Him, and if we don't love our neighbour, we reject the Absolute which is present in that person. This vision helped Kasyan to understand that by giving food to those in need, to the poor and the hungry, we can earn the love of our heavenly Creator, and by giving food and shelter to the homeless and hapless, we pay homage to our Creator. By feeding His children we pay homage to our heavenly Father, and by despising His children we deprive ourselves of the grace of our heavenly Father.

Kasyan then asked himself another question: is the Absolute present in 'bad' people as well as 'good' people? Kasyan focused his mind and asked the heavenly Creator this question. To his great surprise God's voice came from the depth of his heart: 'I am present in all people, good and bad.'

Kasyan could see, with his inner eyes, the presence of the divine Father in all people. This revelation stood vividly in his memory for a long time. While loving people and helping them, we should at the same time see our heavenly Father in them, and by doing good to others, we serve our heavenly King, our heavenly Father. But if our eyes blur we won't be able to discern the image of our heavenly Father behind the images of other people, and then if we try to help others enthusiastically, we may get lost in the chaotic whirlpool of the delusions of our persona. When doing charity work and helping others, we should never forget the image of our Creator and heavenly Father, which is older than eternity. If we love our Creator, we can love others as well, if our eyes are not blinded and we don't forget His existence. But when we forget Him, our love loses its quality and becomes an earthly love instead of a divine one. If we remember our Creator and love Him, then our love for others will be pure and unselfish, winged and inspired, and will have the qualities of a heavenly love, which is not subject to earthly laws.

A few days later, while Kaysan was immersed in deep meditation, he heard a voice from within which repeated: 'God in me, God in me, God in me...'

Kasyan repeated: 'God in me, God in me, God in me...'

The voice sounded day and night incessantly, as if to remind Kasyan forever that God, for whom he was searching, was indeed inside him, as He abides in every human being, and to search for Him outside of himself was useless.

* * *

Concluding Remarks from the Author

I have studied the theory and the practice of Kriya Yoga in the spirit of the tradition of Hesychasts[4] for many years. This book is an attempt to present the results of my studies in an accessible form to those who wish to dedicate their lives to spiritual growth and find God inside their hearts.

The Kriya technique is one of the most important inner techniques on the spiritual Path, as it is one of few techniques that leads the practitioner firmly towards enlightenment. It also has another quality: Kriya doesn't make severe demands (including sexual demands) on the practitioner, and so married couples can follow the spiritual Path with the help of the Kriya techniques.

In the alchemical tradition, the Kriya technique can be applied to all the stages of alchemical transformation.

When a disciple works on the transformation of his or her materia prima, that is the uroboros, Kriya should be exercised for 14 minutes in the morning and in the evening. Disciples should further exercise the techniques to regain the energy which was lost in the past; the techniques of transforming the horizontal karma and the techniques to purify the soul. For these purposes a practitioner may use various techniques of reconsideration which are described in my book 'The Disciple and the Path.' Regular church visits are also necessary, plus the inward so-called 'prayer of forgiveness'. This prayer releases you from burdening past relationships, as well as those in the present, which hamper your progress on the spiritual Path. In the first stages it's also necessary to practice techniques for the transformation of sexual energy. These practices belong to the Tao tradition and are described in my book 'Tao techniques: Tao alchemy in the Hermetic tradition'.

In the next stages of alchemical transformation, the above-mentioned techniques become auxiliary techniques. Kriya techique becomes the principal technique which allows the consciousness of an adept to grow and perceive the divine revelations.

In the alchemical stage called alchemical marriage, the Kriya technique should be exercised daily for at least forty minutes a day.

In the alchemical stage called nigredo, Kriya should be exercised for at least one hour a day.

In the alchemical stage called albedo, the Kriya technique should be exercised for at least two hours a day.

In the alchemical stage called the stage of iridescent colours, the Kriya technique should be exercised for at least three hours a day.

In the alchemical stage called rubedo, the Kriya technique should be exercised for at least four hours a day. The more elevated the stage of alchemical transformation, the longer the Kriya practice should be. By doing this, practitioners are ensured that they will reach enlightenment during their present incarnation.

Konstantin Serebrov
Moscow, May 2007

Endnotes

1 Chistka: hundreds of thousands of members of the Communist Party were thrown into concentration camps or executed in the 1930's. . It was a planned action of Stalin in order to place his own people in key positions.
2 Samizdat: an abbreviation which means literally translated 'self-published'. In common usage it means all kinds of books which were prohibited in the Soviet Union, and which were copied and distributed in all possible ways by the people themselves.
3 Staretz: a spiritual mentor in the Russian Orthodox tradition. The word literally means 'an elder'.
4. Hesychasts: the practitioners of the mystical practices of the so-called 'desert', or 'holy fathers', which were restored in Byzantium in the 14th century by Saint Gregorius Palama

Books by Konstantin Serebrov

Trilogy "Lessons of Master G"
1. Follow Me
2. Live Three Incarnations in One
3. On the Path of alchemical Fusion

Appendix to the Trilogy 'Lessons of Master G'
'Adventures of Master G and his faithful disciples Morose and Bitumen in the Nigredo Valley, or Modern Alchemy. Phantasmagoria'

The series "Alchemical Teachings"
1. Practical Alchemy
2. Spiritual Alchemy in Words and Pictures

The series "Inner Light"
1. The Doctrine of inner Light
2. Spiritual Breath: the Practice of Kriya Yoga

The series "Inner Christianity"
1. Pray and work (on Yourself), Part I
2. Pray and work (on Yourself), part II
3. The 22 Mysteries of the Christian Way

www.ingramcontent.com/pod-product-compliance
Lightning Source LLC
LaVergne TN
LVHW041533070526
838199LV00046B/1647